Marital Separation

Kathy,

Hope this helps

somaund

Juan.

Marital Separation in Contemporary Ireland

Women's Experiences

Lucy Hyland

PETER LANG

Oxford • Bern • Berlin • Bruxelles • Frankfurt am Main • New York • Wien

Bibliographic information published by Die Deutsche Nationalbibliothek.
Die Deutsche Nationalbibliothek lists this publication in the Deutsche National-
bibliografie; detailed bibliographic data is available on the Internet at
http://dnb.d-nb.de.

A catalogue record for this book is available from the British Library.

Library of Congress Control Number: 2015955235

This publication was supported by a bursary from Carlow College.

Cover image: © Stephanie McDermott.

ISBN 978-3-0343-1836-5 (print)
ISBN 978-3-0353-0794-8 (eBook)

© Peter Lang AG, International Academic Publishers, Bern 2016
Hochfeldstrasse 32, CH-3012 Bern, Switzerland
info@peterlang.com, www.peterlang.com, www.peterlang.net

This publication has been peer reviewed.

Printed in Germany

This book is dedicated to the memory of my sister Mary Nolan
(1951–2006)

Contents

Tables

Acknowledgements

First and foremost, I would like to thank the fourteen women who told me their stories of separation. My hope is that I have done them justice and that together we have drawn attention to what was a previously unseen and poorly understood aspect of Irish women's lives.

I wish to express my sincere thanks to my students and colleagues at Carlow College for their on-going assistance and encouragement. I would like to thank my supervisor, Dr Jacqui O'Riordan, for her guidance throughout the writing of the original dissertation. I would also like to thank the staff and students of the School of Applied Social Studies in UCC, for their support throughout the DSocSc programme.

This book could not have been completed without the support of my family and friends. I would like to thank my brother James for his help with proof-reading and for his invaluable feedback and advice. I would like to thank my brothers, Pat and William, for always being at the end of a phone if I needed them. I would like to thank my two children, Fiona and Jack, who had to live with me through the ups and downs that have been my life for the past seven years. I would like to thank my friends who have continued to stay in touch and to help me in so many ways. I have drawn huge strength from knowing that my sister, my mother, my father and my friend Kay O'Reilly would all have been proud of me if they had lived to see me complete this book.

CHAPTER I

Introduction

On Easter Sunday morning, the 23rd March 2008, I discovered that my husband was having an affair. After a marriage that had lasted for twenty-four years, he moved out of our home permanently one week later. This is obviously not the whole story but, for our children's sake, it is as much as I am prepared to tell right now. The following November I attended two post-separation courses in Dublin. Neither course was advertised as being solely for women or as being specifically for women aged over forty-five years of age, but that is who was there. It occurred to me that there was something taking place across the country about which very little had been written or was known and which warranted further study.

I had started a Doctorate in Social Science (DSocSc) at University College Cork (UCC) in September 2007. For a period after my separation, the only topic I was able to focus on making sense of was marital separation, so that became the subject of my dissertation. This book is based on interviews with fourteen women who had separated which I carried out in July and August of 2010 as part of my doctoral dissertation.

Irish Context

The most recent figures published by the Central Statistics Office (CSO, September 2012) show that in 2011 a total of 115,046 women were either separated or divorced in Ireland. The CSO report (2012) also states that 'the rate of separation begins to increase when people are in their late twenties and increases steadily throughout the thirties and forties, reaching a peak at age forty-eight' (p. 9). These figures confirm that separation currently affects a considerable number of people in Ireland and that it is predominantly a midlife phenomenon, affecting people mainly in their forties and fifties.

The age group of women with which this book is concerned consti-tutes the first generation of Irish women to separate openly in such large numbers. Women who are currently in midlife will have entered marriage at a time when divorce was illegal in Ireland. It is likely they will have been socialised to believe in lifelong marriage. They are the first generation of Irish women to experience such a public change in the structure of their mar-riages and of their families. There is no clear cultural script for the manner in which Irish women should experience separation. How this age cohort of women make sense of and feel about separation will not be the same as for women in other countries or, possibly, even for later generations of Irish women. It is important therefore to give voice to these women now.

Aims and Rationale

The aim of this book is to contribute towards a greater understanding of Irish women's experiences of separation. Almost no research has been done into this specific topic. The book is written by an 'insider' and provides an 'insider's' view of what separation is like as described by fourteen Irish women who are separated. It will deal not only with legal, housing and financial aspects but also with the range of emotions that accompany the events and the processes involved in separating.

The book is written primarily in an academic style, using theoretical concepts, references and quotations from academic literature. It is written mainly from a sociological perspective but every effort is made to make the work accessible to as wide an audience as possible. Verbatim quotations from the fourteen women constitute the bulk of the writing. This material will be of interest to women and men who are separating, to their children, their families and friends. It will provide useful insights for students of families and to the wide range of practitioners and policy makers whose job it is to support families.

Marital separation 'is a metaphorical surgery which effects all areas of life of the individual' (Satir, 1980 in Fisher and Alberti, 2008:ix). It has 'the potential to create considerable turmoil in people's lives' (Amato, 2000:1269), hence the need to understand it better and to provide appropriate support. Separation has implications, not just for families with young children, as has been the subject of much recent research (Hogan *et al.*, 2002; Mahon and Moore, 2011) but also for families with older adolescents and young adults. Women who separate in midlife have been found to be at greater risk of poverty (Weston and Smyth, 2000), and many may be living alone (Lunn *et al.*, 2009). These findings are all issues which will have implications for the level of services and supports required by separated women and their families.

Literature on Separation and Divorce

It was very difficult to find studies which dealt specifically with women who separated in midlife. According to Smart (1999), there was some sympathy during the 1960s in the UK for older women whose husbands divorced them, but 'what sympathy there was, quickly evaporated a decade later when they were re-defined as alimony drones and as women who were too idle to work' (p. 8). It is not clear if this lack of sympathy also resulted in a lack of interest by researchers. For whatever reason, there is very little material published on this specific age group of women so the literature search for this study was quickly broadened to include material on separation and divorce which occurred at any age.

Much of the Irish literature referred to in this book deals with the events, structures and ideologies, mainly Catholic ideologies on gender and familism which have shaped Irish women's lives over the past sixty years and have influenced their attitudes to marriage, family and separation (Inglis, 1998, 2003; O'Connor, 1998; Bacik, 2004; Connolly, 2015). A key premise of this study is that the experience of living through the changes from a society in which Catholic familist ideology was dominant to a more liberal society in which there are more choices about how people engage with and structure their families is likely to impact on women who currently separate in Ireland in midlife.

Recent Irish research on separation has tended to focus on children (Hogan *et al.*, 2002; Mahon and Moore, 2011), on legal arrangements (Coulter, 2008) on grandparents (Timonen *et al.*, 2009) and on statistical analyses of rates of separation and divorce (Lunn *et al.*, 2009; CSO, 2012). The issues raised in these studies concern the impact of separation on children, the risk of poverty for women and children following separation, the impact of parental conflict on children and the role of fathers and grandparents in post-separation families. Apart from the reference to the increased risk of poverty for women, there is very little focus specifically on women.

It is not clear why the voices of women who separate have not been heard or why their experiences have been so invisible. It may relate to the invisibility of 'women of a certain age'. Writing in an American context, Bateson (2000) comments on how few stories are told about women in midlife. She suggests that this may be about to change because 'there is a substantial period when many women no longer find the meaning of their lives through their roles as mothers, and do not immediately segue into the grandparent role' (p. 102). It may be that midlife as a life stage was not visible for Irish women in previous generations and that this text too, as well as the script on how to separate, is being written by women in contemporary Ireland.

The international literature on separation and divorce which was reviewed for this study was written from mainly sociological, psychological and practice-oriented perspectives. The sociological studies (e.g. Dronkers *et al.*, 2006; Smart, 2007) largely dealt with the impact of changes in society on marital breakdown. The societal changes identified as contributing to the increased rate of marriage breakdown included globalisation and individualisation (Giddens, 1992; Beck and Beck-Gernsheim, 1995), changing gender roles, women's employment and the removal of barriers to divorce. The psychological literature (e.g. Amato, 2000; Lowenstein, 2007) dealt, in a more linear fashion, with the 'causes' and 'consequences' of divorce. It also dealt with the factors that facilitated or hindered adjustment to divorce. The practice-oriented literature (e.g. Carter and McGoldrick, 2005; Fisher and Alberti, 2006; O'Hara, 2011) dealt with the range of emotions that people experience in their journeys through separation, the stages that are typically involved in the process and the types of support that people need. The clear implication of the combined literature is that separation must be understood as a process which takes time to unfold rather than being seen as a single event.

Amato (2000) summarises the range of consequences of divorce for different people. 'Divorce benefits some individuals, leads others to experience temporary decrements in well-being, and forces others on a downward trajectory from which they may never recover' (p. 1269). As with many potentially stressful events and processes in life, people vary in their responses to separation. At one end of a continuum there are those who are distraught and who may struggle for years, in the middle there are those who feel very upset initially but who recover and cope after a while, and at the other end there are people who feel liberated by separation and divorce. It is important, therefore, not to assume that everyone who goes through it will experience separation in the same way or that there is just one way to think, feel and act.

A key theme in the international literature is that separation should be seen as a transition and not as a failure, as was common in the past (Bateson, 2000; Carter and McGoldrick, 2005). Another theme involves families not being seen as broken or fragmented by separation but as being connected and re-configured in different ways (Smart, 2007). The finding is that people can adapt to this transition and treat it as another chapter in their adult lives (Bateson, 2000). The other suggestion in the literature is that it is preferable if separations can be dealt with in a harmonious manner. Conflict, according to Smart (1999), has been identified as the most damaging aspect of separation, particularly where there are children involved. There has also been increasing interest in and concern that fathers are being excluded from their children's lives. There has been a focus on the implications of trying to achieve equality in post-separation parenting (Trinder, 2008).

The research questions which follow were influenced by the findings from the literature reviewed. The questions address many of the themes identified and attempt to investigate them in an Irish context, particularly as they relate to women.

Research Questions

The overarching question which the study set out to explore is as follows:

What are Irish women's experiences of separation in midlife?

This broad question was broken down into five more specific questions, each dealing with a different aspect of the overall experience.

1. *In what ways do family and cultural attitudes to marital breakdown influence how women in midlife experience separation in Ireland?*

The background to this question was a belief that the experience of separation could only be understood within the context in which it occurred. The question was asked in order to find out how women who were raised in a traditional Catholic society in which divorce was illegal, come to terms with separation/divorce in their own lives.

2. *What are the key contributory processes and events that lead to separation in midlife?*

The background to this question was that separation could not be examined without knowing the events and processes that led up to it. The experience of separation was conceptualised in this study as a process that had a 'before', a 'during' and an 'after'. Based on the findings from the literature reviewed (e.g. Amato, 2000), the approach taken was that separation began long before the actual separation took place, that it included a period when the decision to separate was discussed and arrangements were made to move out and that coming to terms with separation and re-constituting relationships afterwards were all part of the experience and the story of separation.

3. *What losses and gains are experienced as part of the transition through separation?*

The background to this question was that it was important to acknowledge that separation was a journey that people travelled, but that it was also important to draw attention to the losses and the gains that separation entailed along the way, rather than just focusing on the end point of the journey.

4. *In what ways are relationships and family practices re-constructed following separation?*

The background to the fourth question was to begin to explore what changes in family relationships and family practices Irish women were instigating post-separation. Separation in such large numbers is such a relatively new occurrence in Irish families that the question was asked in an attempt to find out what practices were actually taking place in separated families and how relationships with spouses, children, extended families and friends were being re-constructed following separation.

5. *What supports do women find most beneficial when going through the process of separation?*

The objective of this question is to explore the types of support that women find most helpful when dealing with the emotional and practical aspects involved in separation. The answer to this question will guide recommendations for the types of informal and formal support services that need to be provided.

Theoretical Orientation

The book is written primarily from a sociological perspective in that it is concerned with the relationships between individuals and their social context, between Irish women who separate and the society in which they live. Morgan (2002) identifies two broad perspectives within family sociology. One approach sees family as an independent variable which is unique and about which sociology can provide only a partial insight, the main understanding coming from the fields of psychology and biology. The other approach sees family as a dependent variable which is merely a sub-set of society and can be analysed in much the same way as any other social institution. The solution, Morgan (2002) suggests, is to take a 'middle ground' position between the two approaches, to include elements of interpersonal interactions, as well as societal influences, and to emphasise the 'doing' of family practices. Family practices refer to the ordinary, everyday interactions that are part of family life. Family practices include how family members talk to each other, how they exchange resources and services, how they have shared knowledge of each other's lives and needs (Cheal, 2002). This study set out to explore what happens to ordinary, everyday family interactions when a marriage breaks down and spouses no longer live together.

The study is located within current debates in sociology about the continuities and changes in the nature of personal and family relationships (Gillies, 2003; Connolly, 2015). Individualisation theorists (Beck and Beck-Gernsheim, 2002; Giddens, 2006) claim that personal fulfilment and the pursuit of individual goals are the driving force behind current relationship patterns (one of which is marital separation). Empirical researchers (e.g. Smart, 2007), on the other hand, contend that empirical studies do not support the individualisation thesis and that people continue to be influenced by family considerations and continue to show a desire for connectedness, albeit resulting in a diversity of family forms. Both sides of the argument are considered in the analysis of the women's narratives about their separation experiences.

Smart (2007) suggests that theorisation need not be a goal in itself but that theories can provide a 'toolbox' of insights which can be put together in different ways to form a flexible analysis of a topic. Using Smart's approach, a 'tool box' of analytical concepts was assembled. Five separate but related concepts, which are explained below, were used as the lenses through which the data were analysed.

- The concept of 'embeddedness' was used to analyse data on the manner in which attitudes to marriage and separation internalised during child-hood affected how Irish women experienced their own separations.
- The concepts of 'love and care' were used to examine the behaviours and processes around showing love or failing to show love which con-tributed to difficulties in marriages and led to eventual separations.
- The concept of 'transition' was used to capture the series of losses and gains that occurred during the women's journeys through separation.
- The concept of 'identity' was used to examine the shift in identity required as a result of the break-up of a long-term marriage.
- The concept of 'individualisation' was used when considering women's disconnection from 'traditional' beliefs, their motivation for initiating separation and when considering how relationships were re-configured following separation.

Each concept acts like a spotlight to direct attention towards and illuminate one aspect of the overall experience of separation at a time. The pieces are then put together to provide a broader range of insights, leading to a deeper understanding and a clearer 'picture' of the overall experience of separation.

Methodology

Several aspects of the methodology were influenced by feminist perspectives on research. Feminists (e.g. Harding, 1987) argue that, in the past, research was conducted from a male perspective and assumed that male experiences equated to human experience. By focussing primarily on women's experiences, there is an assumption being made that there are gendered aspects to the experience of separation. It is assumed, because of the social construction of gender roles, that women have particular vantage points and perspectives which it is important to understand and to represent as a separate entity. It is acknowledged that, by concentrating solely on women's experiences, only a proportion of the story of separation is being told. Men, children and extended family members are also key actors in this story but are not the primary focus of this study.

A qualitative interpretative approach was used in the study. In-depth interviews of a narrative type were conducted with fourteen women whom I had met at two different post-separation courses in Dublin in November 2009. Each woman was asked to recount, in a more or less chronological order, stories about episodes in her life which were relevant to how she interpreted her separation. The study set out to explore how embedded the women were in both the external (cultural) narratives about marriage and separation in Ireland as well as the internal narratives which were influenced by each woman's relationships and life experience, all of which combined to form a complex account of how the women understood and explained their separations. Using narratives provided a way to explain events in detail, as well as illustrating the meaning of events, the feelings that accompanied events and how people made sense in retrospect of events (Mason, 2002).

The interviews took place in locations that were most suitable for the women. In most cases I travelled to their homes. Where this was not suitable because of children being at home, interviews took place in hotels or work places. The interviews typically lasted between eighty and one hundred and twenty minutes. Each interview was tape recorded. Transcripts of the interviews and excerpts from this book were sent to each woman for their approval prior to including them in this text.

The data are not presented as fourteen individual case studies, but are analysed under the key themes in the research questions. The intention was to capture commonalities or divergences in the women's accounts, rather than to analyse individual case histories. A thematic framework (Appendix 1) was deduced from the interview transcripts and provides the headings under which the data are discussed and analysed. Direct quotations constitute the bulk of the data presented. It was not possible to present quotations from each of the fourteen women on each topic. Representative quotations were chosen which reflect the range of responses to the questions posed. Every effort was made to ensure that the women's voices were heard. My voice will undoubtedly also be heard but, as stated at the start, this is not my story. May (2002) claims that researchers can use their understanding as a starting point from which to push on and learn more. They can both utilise and challenge their own understanding as they engage in a reflexive style of conducting research. This is the approach I have attempted to adopt in this study. I have both utilised and challenged my own experience of separation by reading widely on the topic and by listening to and representing accurately what fourteen different women had to say about their experiences.

It is acknowledged that the small size of the sample means that findings cannot be generalised to a larger population. The only claim that is being made is that this study represents the views of fourteen separated Irish women and offers an insight into the complexity and diversity of their experiences of separation. The book is structured around answering each of the research questions in turn. It takes a life course or chronological approach and describes events, emotions and outcomes at each stage of the process of separation. The strength of the study lies in the richness of the data collected. The data provide a base from which to begin to explore further what separation is like for Irish women and their families.

Terms Used

The term 'separation' refers simply to the decision to end a marriage and to live separately. Prior to divorce being legalised in Ireland in 1997, many couples separated but could not divorce. Under current Irish divorce legislation a couple must be separated for four of the previous five years before a divorce can be granted (Nestor, 2006). Separation is, therefore, a significant part of the experience of marital breakdown in Ireland. Some of the participants in the study had proceeded to divorce but the focus was primarily on their experiences during separation.

'Experience' is defined in the phenomenological sense of 'lived experience'. This encompasses trying to capture both the emotional and practical aspects of separation, as well as the processes and events that make up the experience and have implications for women's identity following separation. As stated already, a basic assumption of the study is that separation is a gendered experience and will be perceived somewhat differently by men and women. However, there is no assumption that separation will be experienced in the same way by all women, or even by all Irish women who are in midlife. The challenge is to represent accurately the diversity of experience that the primary data contains.

There is no agreement in the literature on when 'midlife' begins or when it ends. It is variously defined as starting between thirty-five (Bogolub, 1991) and forty years of age (Uhlenberg *et al.*, 1990; Montenegro *et al.*, 2004) and ending between fifty-five and sixty years of age. For the purposes of this study, midlife is defined as being between forty-five and fifty-nine years of age, as this represents the age range of the participants in the study.

CHAPTER 2

Childhood

This chapter presents the data and discussion on the early years of the women's lives. It is concerned with beginning to answer the first research question about the influence of being raised in Ireland in the 1950s and 1960s on later experiences of separation. To begin with, the concept of embeddedness, which is the main concept used to analyse the data in this section, will be introduced. Then the data will be presented, mainly in the form of direct quotations from the women. In order not to distract from the flow of the quotations, the discussion piece will be located at the end of the chapter.

Embeddedness is a concept which denotes deep connection. It denotes a phenomenon which permeates key aspects of an individual's personality and which influences important aspects of their behaviour. Smart (2007) outlines 'the importance of always putting the individual in the context of their past, their web of relationships, their possessions and their sense of location' (p. 45). She talks about how family embeddedness can be experienced, on the one hand, as providing ontological security (security about a person's place in the world) or, on other hand, as being suffocating. In this study, embeddedness relates to the ways in which women are connected to their families of origin and are influenced by the values and attitudes of family members. It relates to the extent to which women are influenced by and embedded in Irish values, beliefs and attitudes towards marriage and separation, many of which were inculcated during childhood years.

Childhood

This section begins by presenting a table containing background details
with regard to the fourteen women who were interviewed for this study.
Each woman was allocated a pseudonym. Occupations and locations are
described in very broad terms in order to ensure anonymity. The chapter
will describe aspects of the women's early lives and what they identified as
the key influences during childhood on their understanding of marriage
and marital separation. It will set the scene for discussions on the ways
in which the women were embedded in socio-cultural norms regarding
women and the place of marriage and family in women's lives (O'Hara,
1997; Inglis, 1998, 2003: O'Connor, 1998).

Table 1: Profiles of the Women during their Childhood Years

Name	Location	*Father's Occupation	Mother's Occupation	Number of Children	Religion	Education prior to Marriage
Anne	Rural	Non-manual	Housewife	7	Catholic	Third level
Breda	City	Skilled manual	Housewife	5	Catholic	Inter Cert
Catherine	City	Non-manual	Housewife	3	Catholic	One year at third level
Deirdre	Rural	Farmer	Teacher	4	Catholic	Third level
Eileen	Town	Professional	Housewife	7	Catholic	Third level
Frances	City	Professional	Housewife	5	Catholic	Third level
Geraldine	City	Non-manual	Housewife	2	Catholic	Second level
Helen	City	Non-manual	Housewife	3	Catholic	Second level
Irene	Rural	Farmer/ Shop keeper	Shop keeper	5	Catholic	Third level

Name	Location	*Father's Occupation	Mother's Occupation	Number of Children	Religion	Education prior to Marriage
Jane	City	Skilled Manual	Housewife	4	Catholic	Second level
Kay	Rural	Professional /farmer	Housewife/ farmer	7	Catholic	Third level
Sarah	City	Non-manual	Shopkeeper	5	Catholic	Third level
Mary	City	Non-manual	Housewife	9	Catholic	Third level
Nora	Rural	Skilled manual	Housewife	7	Catholic	Inter Cert

*Examples given on next page

Family of Origin Details

Table 1 introduces the fourteen women who were interviewed for this study. All of the women were born and raised in Ireland, as were their parents. The women were born between 1952 and 1963. Half of them spent their childhoods in Dublin, four grew up on farms in Cork, Louth, Leitrim and Galway and the remaining three lived in urban areas in Offaly, Kildare and Waterford. Eleven of the fourteen participants came from families that had between four and nine children. Families of this size would have been the norm in the 1950s and 1960s in Ireland but would have been considered large by international standards (Fahey and Field, 2008).

During all of the women's early childhoods, their parents were married and living together, none had died or were separated. A number of studies show a link between parents being divorced and their children going on to divorce (Kavas and Gunduz-Hosgor, 2011). No such link was possible in Ireland given that divorce was banned until 1997. Two of the women mentioned that their husbands' parents were separated. Two women said that were alcohol and related problems in their families of origin. Other women stated that there were problems with relationships in their husbands' families but, apart from the two mentioned, no separations. It was beyond the scope of this study to enquire into individual family issues which might be linked to separating later in life. At a public level at any rate, all of the women came from 'intact' families. They came largely from 'mainstream' as opposed to 'problem' families.

Eleven of the women described their mothers as full-time mothers and housewives. This is in line with Clear's (2001) statement that in Ireland in 1961, 93.7% of married women were 'engaged in home duties' (p. 18). Clear uses the phrase 'women of the house' to refer to women who 'had primary responsibility for the daily maintenance of a dwelling and of the lives of its members, through gathering and preparing food, organising the living space, looking after clothing, and often physically and culturally reproducing – bearing and rearing children – in addition to this work' (Clear, 2001: 12). This is the model of wife and mother that eleven of the women in this study grew up with. Of the other three mothers, one was a teacher and two were shopkeepers. These, again, are occupations identified as important exceptions to the rule that mothers did not work outside the home. Clear (2001) states that the midwife, the teacher, the shopkeeper and the postmistress were important, independent, authoritative female figures in communities.

The fathers' occupations included three skilled manual workers (fitters and electricians), six non-manual workers (clerks, postmen and salesmen), three professionals (medics, engineers and civil servants) and two farmers. Some of the men had two occupations; teaching as well as farming, running a shop or working in construction as well as farming. As a general rule, different standards of living for families related to fathers' occupations. The majority of the families described in this study would have been considered to have been relatively well-off by the standards of the day.

In most cases the family backgrounds followed a traditional male breadwinner model with the husband out at work and his wife at home taking care of the children and engaging in household and farm duties. This model had religious (which will be discussed in the next section) as well as legislative support. Article 41 of the 1937 Constitution (*Bunreacht na hÉireann*, 1937, Article 41) enshrined the importance of the family and of women's role within the family as follows: The State guarantees 'to guard with special care the institution of marriage, on which the Family is founded' (Article 41.3.1). This Article also 'recognises that by her life within the home, woman gives to the State a support without which the common good cannot be achieved' (Article 41.2.1). It states further that the state shall 'endeavour to ensure that mothers shall not be obliged by economic necessity to engage in labour to the neglect of their duties in the home' (Article 41.2.2). These Articles set the context in which the 'male breadwinner model' of family life is seen as the norm. In this model, the man, while not visible in the above wording, is the patriarch who goes out to work to provide for his family and the woman is a full-time housewife and mother whose role is to take care of her husband and children.

Legislative support for a 'male breadwinner model' in families was also shown in 'the marriage ban' which was introduced in 1933. This ban prevented women from working in the civil service, local authorities, banks and health boards once they got married and stayed in effect until 1973. There was a clear government policy, which seems to have been supported by the majority of the people, given how little opposition there was when the 'ban' was being introduced, to prevent married women from working outside the home (Clear, 2001). This meant that available work was for men and for single women. It was not established how many of the women's mothers had had to give up jobs when they got married. What was established was that eleven out of the fourteen women described their mothers' full-time occupation as 'housewife' which was in keeping with the gender roles of the time in Ireland.

Catholic Upbringing

The notion of embeddedness in Catholicism, prevalent during their childhoods and as part of their socialisation and education, is key to understanding the experience of Irish women who are now in midlife and who are separated. What was common to all the women in the study was that they were all raised as Catholics but, in this respect too, there were variations in the extent to which they felt their parents were influenced by the Catholic Church. Families ranged along a continuum from those who were very traditionally Catholic, 'country Catholic' as Sarah calls them in a later quotation, with priests and nuns in the extended family to those who went to Mass on Sundays but were otherwise not 'religious in any way' (Irene). Two of the women (Breda and Sarah) stated that they had Protestant grandparents which, they thought, resulted in more liberal views about religion in their particular families, as Breda explains;

> BREDA: There is a kind of paradox in that they were very Catholic but my mother's mother was a Methodist and that was a different influence.

Anne's family clearly fits into a very traditional Catholic category;

> ANNE: They were very religious. He had two sisters who were nuns and they were very much 'what the church said was law'. My mother wasn't as strict. I think she could see there were flaws in it but of course she went along with whatever her husband said. That was the way, but she wouldn't have been 'dyed in the wool', she wouldn't have been ruled by it so much, whereas my father's family were very traditional and as a result, they passed on a very strong faith to me. I am not really a traditional Catholic now but I do have a strong faith and I think that has come from my background and my family.

Anne was clearly aware that, even between her parents, there were differences in adherence to Catholic beliefs. She could see that her mother had some reservations about the dominance of the Catholic Church but that, in keeping with the patriarchal thinking at the time, her mother publically supported her husband's views. Anne explains her father's devotion by the fact that he had so many relations who were nuns and priests. His family were deeply embedded in Catholicism and his children were expected to live by the same moral code. Family affiliation took precedence over individual beliefs about a range of matters, including religion.

Sarah tells a different story about the place of formal Catholic practices in her house when she was growing up.

> SARAH: They weren't holy, holies, like Mom wouldn't go to Mass every day. They'd be religious, like going on Sundays ... but there was no saying the rosary, there were no holy pictures, statues. There would have been one or two nice little china statues, but no chalky big statues. She got rid of the Sacred Heart picture. Not any of what

> I would think as country Catholic. Dad's family was Protestant originally, and his mother converted, Mom's being inner city Dublin, kind of, it was Catholic, but not country Catholic, you know.

Sarah went on to marry a man who was 'country Catholic' so she was acutely aware of the differences in how central traditional religious practices were in his family compared to her family. Irene and Nora similarly describe adherence to Catholic practices in their families but, in retrospect, they did not consider their parents to be 'overly religious'

> IRENE: Well, we went to Mass. We had our Sunday best. Mam did knitting and made our dresses. We went to confession on Saturdays.

> NORA: They'd be pretty religious. Well, we said the rosary every night and you went to Confessions every Saturday and Mass every Sunday and that. But, we wouldn't be overly religious.

The key point is that all of the women were brought up in families who were practising Catholics, in the sense that they all went to Mass on Sundays. Their stories show differences in the extent to which Catholicism dominated their daily lives. For some, being a Catholic involved going to Mass on Sundays (and being educated by nuns, as discussed below). For others, particularly those brought up in rural areas, Catholic practices, Catholic images and Catholic priests and nuns were defining aspects of their family lives and in their families' status in the community.

Access to Education

Twelve of the fourteen women attended Catholic, single-sex secondary schools. The remaining two (Anne and Nora) attended vocational schools. Two of the women (Breda and Nora) left school at fifteen and sixteen respectively, having completed their Intermediate Certificate.[1] The

---

1   The Intermediate Certificate is a State examination which is completed after three years of second-level education.

remainder completed Leaving Certificate.[2] Three of the sample (Eileen, Frances and Irene) attended boarding schools. Seven (Anne, Catherine, Deirdre, Frances, Kay, Sarah and Mary) proceeded directly to third-level education following secondary school. Four (Deirdre, Frances, Kay and Sarah) of the seven who went to third-level came from families in which one of their parents had also been to third-level education.

Most of the women spoke positively about their experience of school during the 1960s and 1970s.

> KAY: I went to a single sex, girls' convent school. It was fine. I enjoyed it. I really liked it. Got a bus in every day, I wasn't particularly sporty, the school didn't have many facilities like that, but we did well, it was a pleasant school, we liked going there and we felt we were liked by the teachers.

Different subjects were deemed as being more suitable for girls. Sport was clearly not seen as a priority in Kay's school. Mahon (1994) stated that building women's moral strength was a key objective of religious run-education. The presumption seems to have been that girls would be expected to uphold high moral standards within their families. They would be responsible for getting their children and husbands to attend Mass on a Sunday.

Some of the women were at school in 1966 when 'free' secondary education was announced. Prior to 1966, fees had been charged for attendance at secondary school. They also remembered the advent of free school transportation in 1967. This was a scheme whereby any child who lived more than three miles from their nearest school was entitled to free bus transport to school. Anne, who was the youngest in a family of eight and the only one to go to university in 1978, talked about how opportunities for education opened up for her but had not been available for her older siblings.

> ANNE: My older brothers and sisters had to go to work and did not get a chance to get educated. We were in such a rural area and there was no transport or anything much. Where we lived was quite working class and a lot of the girls wouldn't have been educated. A lot of them would have worked in factories so even to get as far as

---

2   The Leaving Certificate is a State examination taken by students on completion of second-level education.

secretarial course was good for my sisters. By the time I came along, the transport was there so I was able to go to school and then I had a wonderful teacher. Only for her I wouldn't have gone to third level because my family didn't know anything about it really.

Anne was very aware of how unusual it was for girls from rural working class backgrounds to get an opportunity to attend third level education. She was very grateful to a teacher in her vocational school who had given her the confidence and encouragement to attend college.

Mary, who was also the youngest of a large family and grew up in Dublin, told a similar story to Anne.

> MARY: I'm the only person in my family who went to third level, I'm the only person I knew in my whole entire neighbourhood who went to third level. Most people left school after the Junior Cert[3] or Inter Cert as it was then, if even that. My father believed in education. I've no idea where he got it from but his view was that his father was a manual worker, he was an office worker, and he wanted all of us to progress and he believed the way to do that was through education. When my older brothers and sisters started school there was no free education so they would all have had to get scholarships. By the time I came to go to secondary they had just introduced free education but the school I went to was private and it never became public. My father insisted that I had to go to that school so there were some scholarships available and by then my older sisters were working and some of them helped to pay the fees. After he died one of my older sisters paid the fees for the last couple of years.

It is apparent from these extracts that the women lived through a period of significant economic and social change. The Irish economy was shifting from an almost total reliance on agriculture and was opening up to foreign markets and to foreign industrial investment. Education needed to expand to provide a more highly skilled work force. Additional state support began to be given to 'brighter' students from poorer backgrounds to encourage them to remain on in school. Anne's teacher and Mary's father were clearly aware of the importance of a good education as a pathway to availing of the increased opportunities that developments in the economy provided.

3   The Junior Certificate replaced the Intermediate Certificate.

Mary's father also seems to have felt that better opportunities would follow from attending more prestigious schools.

The women were conscious of having increased educational opportunities because they could compare their experience to the experience of their older siblings. Anne was aware that her older brothers and sisters had to leave school and go to work at an earlier age than her. It is interesting to note the expectation in Mary's house that older siblings would provide financial support to help fund the education of a younger sibling. The expectation seems to have been that once adult children were earning that they were obliged to share their income with others in the family if the need arose. Obligation to help other family members seems to have been a taken-for-granted aspect of Irish family living at the time.

Another common theme in stories of family life and childhood in Ireland of the 1950s and 1960s was the theme of emigration. Watching older siblings and, in some cases, parents leave home to look for work or training opportunities (e.g. nursing training) formed part of the history of many families due to the scarcity of opportunities for poorer people in Ireland at the time. Nora spoke about how her brother and sisters had emigrated to England at a young age and how two of her sisters had subsequently settled in England. Having some family members in England is a common scenario in many families, the impact of which will be discussed later when discussing the women's own experiences of living abroad.

The women were conscious that there was a class bias in the Irish education system. The clearest indicator of the change in opportunities that occurred was that this cohort of women could remain on at secondary school and some of them were the first ones, not only in their families but also in their neighbourhoods to attend third level education. Looking back, they were aware of living through a period of social change in which they were lucky enough to be able to avail of greater educational opportunities than had been available in Ireland for previous generations of their families and localities.

Attitudes to Marital Separation

In order to gain an understanding of what separation meant to the women, it was important to gather information about the attitudes to separation that they had encountered during childhood. When the women were asked what knowledge they had of separation when they were growing up, they were unanimous in saying that they had almost no knowledge of it and, because they knew nobody who was separated, the topic of separation never even came up for discussion in their homes or in their schools. This was almost the only point during the entire fourteen interviews about which all of the women were so definite and so unanimous.

> L: What was the attitude to separation in your house when you were growing up?
> FRANCES: It was never spoken about. We didn't know anybody that was separated at all so it never really arose.
> L: You had no cousins, aunts or neighbours separated?
> FRANCES: No, none at all. It never featured. It didn't exist. We had no reason to discuss it.

> IRENE: I don't think I knew it existed. Everybody had a Mammy and a Daddy. If there was separation or divorce, it was associated with the films. There certainly wasn't anybody I knew at all.

> HELEN: There was never anybody that you knew separated. That was the time in Ireland. It was never discussed. It never came into anything.
> L: Was that to do with religious beliefs?
> HELEN: No, I don't think so. My father would have a huge sense of family. He loves family, being a united family was always instilled in us. That type of family values was always very strong.

For Frances, Irene and Helen separation did not exist during childhood. They knew nobody who was separated. As can be seen in the following quotation, Kay was aware, even as a child, that separation was a subject that adults were uncomfortable talking about and that it was a taboo topic of conversation.

KAY: My parents didn't feel comfortable talking about it at all. There was one man who came to dinner once, and I remember all through the meal he was teased. He wore a beard, and 'kissing a man with a beard was like salt' something like that. And they were so embarrassed afterwards when they discovered that actually he was separated. But the people who brought him obviously didn't feel comfortable telling them he was separated, so I'd say it was a big, big thing.

This quotation shows the level of silence and unease around separation. The man who was brought to visit did not volunteer the information that he was separated, presumably because he understood that it was a taboo subject. The adults who teased him about kissing women presumably, would not have been so indelicate as to suggest that he would kiss anyone, if they had known that he was no longer living with/kissing his wife.

However, awareness of marriages that everybody knew to be unhappy was referred to by several of the women. They were aware of parents who lived in different parts of a house. They knew of families in which one parent 'lived abroad' but the word 'separated' was not mentioned.

KAY: We heard of a neighbour, again we only heard of it afterwards, his daughter was in my class, and he was from the same area as my father, so there was a connection. They used to visit, and the daughter in my class got anorexia. We discovered years afterwards that the father and mother actually lived in separate rooms in the house.

It is not clear if Kay was connecting the fact that the daughter got anorexia to her parents' marital difficulties or if she was just commenting on how it was possible to not know that a couple who were fairly regular visitors to her home in fact seldom spoke to each other and were living in separate sections of their house. Kay's memory of that incident relates to an earlier time during her secondary school days. She referred to a similar example of a girl she met years later when they were in college together.

KAY: I remember meeting a girl in college whose father lived in England fifty weeks of the year and came home two weeks in the summer, and the week at Christmas. She never said ...

What the women seemed to be stressing was that unhappy marriages had always existed, at a private level, just that the threshold at which a separation could be triggered in the past was extremely high. The expectation was that people stayed together no matter what difficulties they encountered and if they did separate for a while, efforts would be made to get them back together again or else they hid the fact that they were separated, as shown above.

> EILEEN: I remember my mother had one friend whose marriage was very difficult. I was aware that some marriages were very difficult ... but there was no separation. People just stayed together, they stayed together. They had this marriage certificate that said 'til death do us part', regardless of what occurred.

> CATHERINE: None of my parents' friends were separated. I had one cousin who was separated for a while but they got back together.

There also seems to have been a suggestion that there was something wrong, something deviant or different about someone that separated, as the following extract illustrates:

> GERALDINE: My mother has a god-child and she separated from her husband (when I was young). My mother was devastated. She was broken hearted. She took it nearly personally but afterwards when my mother was telling my father about it, it was more or less 'well, she wasn't a very strong person. She was always a bit flighty'. They thought he was lovely. They thought he was a particularly nice man and 'you know, it's an awful shame that that happened but she was a bit of a flighty character'. She wasn't a very settled sort of person.

There seems to be an insinuation that the couple separated because the woman was not morally strong. The onus for the breakdown of the marriage appears to have been on the woman. This may have been accurate in this case, but as a general rule Bateson (2000) suggests that women have to 'deal with the cultural bias that suggests that the termination of any marriage is a failure on the woman's part' (p. 28).

Another theme that emerged was that separation was something that happened to non-Irish people who lived here or in other countries, possibly to celebrities or to Irish people that lived abroad.

EILEEN: There was an English student whose parents were separated but that wasn't ever spoken about either. Because she was English, it didn't have any effect on us at all.

GERALDINE: Any of the celebrities (it didn't happen to us or people like us) or any of the people on the news who were divorcing or separating, they were frowned upon. It really was frowned upon and it wasn't the done thing. My father was quite religious, he was very staunch. They are extremely zealous Catholics, if you like. My father used to always say, not just about marriage but about anything 'if you join, you must soldier.' So no matter what you signed up to and particularly if you signed up to Holy Matrimony, you stuck with it. As far as he was concerned, and my mother as well (they had more or less the same view), they frowned on it.

KAY: Both my parents had brothers and sisters whose marriages had broken down abroad, but they were not referred to, ever. And in one case where my mother's brother's marriage (had broken down), it happened just for a year or two and then they got back together, she refused to admit it was happening, and when we spoke to her about it (we were in our twenties then) she still refused to talk about it. It was too big a thing. It was a major failure. And that was the one time we tackled her because my uncle came home with his daughter, and his daughter said: 'you know my Mom and Dad are separated' and we hadn't known. It just wasn't mentioned. And when you tried to say it to her, she practically told us that the daughter was telling us lies. She didn't want to talk about it.

These extracts show that the women were very clear that the message they had been given during their childhood was that separation was something 'horrific'. It was too awful to talk about. It only happened in Hollywood or to non-Irish (non-Catholic?) people living here. It certainly did not happen in 'respectable' Irish families and if it did happen, it often was not spoken about or it was denied. There was a clear stigma attached to separation. It was so awful that it had to be kept secret and those who tried to discuss its existence in their families were silenced. Being Irish, Catholic and from a 'good' family meant that you did not separate.

Jane stated that she had only just made the connection during the interview between how upset she felt about her separation and the manner in which she had heard separation discussed during her childhood.

JANE: I was in primary school and it was two girls in the class; one girl's mother went off with this girl's father, and to me, my God! And to this day I still look at these people and think that that was horrific, but that's gas, because looking at them now maybe that had a lot to do with the way I felt when my husband left, that the whole town was talking about me. It was so horrific back then, the shame of it. Now that's only after dawning on me now. That's the connection I'm only after making, talking to you now.

Jane is giving a very clear answer to the research question about how being raised in Ireland influenced how she experienced her separation years later. Her answer is emphatically in the affirmative.

Discussion: Embeddedness in Family and Religion during Childhood

The Catholic Church is widely recognised as having played a significant role in shaping ideology about gender and family in Ireland (O'Connor, 1998; Connolly, 2003; Bacik, 2004; Inglis, 2005; Connolly, 2015). It is suggested that the Church influenced women on several levels (O'Connor, 1998): it influenced women through its involvement in the educational system and through the rituals of Mass and the Catholic sacraments. It also influenced women's lives through its shaping of the laws that were enacted by the state, as already shown in the extracts quoted from the 1937 Constitution and in the discussion on the 'marriage ban'.

When the women who participated in this study were growing up, the teachings of the Catholic Church on women, on family life and on marriage were the dominant values transmitted to Catholic children both at home and in school. Mahon (1994) argues that 'a church controlled educational system facilitated both social integration and socialisation into Catholic norms and values' (p. 1278). Socialisation into a Catholic ethos was implemented in schools through staffing, symbols, the physical environment and through the curriculum (Tovey and Share, 2000). Teachers were trained in religious run sex-segregated teacher training colleges and the nuns and priests who ran these colleges 'looked for a strong Catholic ethos in applicants, most of whom came from rural backgrounds where Catholic values were strongest' (Mahon, 1994:1279). Staff members were expected to adhere to a Catholic ethos both in their teaching and in their private lives, as the case of Eileen Flynn illustrates.

Eileen Flynn was sacked from her position as a secondary school teacher in Wexford in 1982, because she was unmarried with a baby son and was living with the child's father, who was a separated man (Holland, 1985). She lost a legal case for unlawful dismissal. The judge ruled that the religious order was within its rights to dismiss the teacher on the basis that the order had a right to operate in a manner which was consistent with the ethos of the school and in line with their religious beliefs (Holland, 1985). Eileen had openly breached a code for 'respectable' women which forbade pre-marital sex, unmarried motherhood, cohabitation and having a relationship with a married man.

Religiously symbolic holy pictures and statues adorned the walls of corridors and classrooms. Classes began and ended with a prayer. Ten per cent of the timetable was allocated to religion (Mahon, 1994:1279). Preparation for the key childhood sacraments of First Holy Communion[4] and Confirmation[5] took place within school time and were an integral part of the school year, as well as marking an exit from primary school, as in the case of Confirmation.

While the religious educators may have passed on traditional moral values to the girls in their care, there is no sense that they took the education of girls less seriously than the education of boys (Clear, 2001). Mahon (1994) suggests that 'the education of girls was equally important as the education of boys, as their spiritual welfare was important' (p. 1281). However, as seen in some of the quotations, gendered ideologies were apparent in that girls were geared towards more 'female' subjects, like domestic science

---

4   Holy Communion is one of seven sacraments that Catholics may receive during their lifetimes. First Holy Communion is a ceremony which signifies that a child has reached the use of reason, thereby knowing right from wrong. It is generally received for the first time when a child is seven or eight years of age.

5   Confirmation is another of the seven sacraments within the Catholic Church. This sacrament is generally administered to a young person at the age of twelve or thirteen years. Confirmation marks the transition, by way of a ceremony, to early adulthood.

and typing, and occupations such as nursing, teaching and secretarial work. On the one hand, girls were educated to enter the world of work, on the other hand they were socialised to be 'guardians of the moral order, to be unselfish and non-assertive (Lynch, 1988:27). Marriage and family were seen as central to women's lives.

Reflecting on forty years of feminism, Mary Kenny (2003) wonders whether 'some aspects of feminism were the continuous and direct result of convent education' (p. 8). She suggests that Mother Superiors[6] represented powerful female role models who were in charge of managing 'great estates and in effect international corporations' (p. 8). The drawback was that in order to achieve this elevated status, girls had to be unmarried and celibate (O'Connor, 1998) and live somewhat apart from the community and their families. Becoming a nun was not an option chosen by any of the women in the study, although several of them did follow the example of the nuns in becoming teachers.

Irish girls, unlike girls in some countries, had equal access to education and were expected to work at their studies and encouraged to do well in exams (Kenny, 2003). It is argued that while there was a gender bias in education, as also shown in several of the quotations from the women, there was an even more significant class bias (O'Connor, 1998; Lynch, 1999). Lynch (1999) highlighted 'very significant differences in patterns of achievement across social groups' (p. 171). Although, change was beginning to happen.

The notion of embeddedness in Catholicism, particularly during their childhoods, is key to understanding the experience of the women who participated in this study. In the 1950s and 1960s, messages about how to be a good girl and later a good wife and mother were 'inculcated in the way the Church represented women, the way mothers raised their daughters, the way girls were taught in schools, and the way women enforced the

---

6   A Mother Superior is a nun in charge of a religious congregation of women who live under vows within the Catholic Church. Hill (2009) states 'nuns often monopolized the senior positions of hospital matrons or secondary school principal within the Catholic community' (p. 47).

message to each other' (Inglis, 2003: 137). The messages for girls were predominantly about the virtues of self-denial. Mothers, in particular, at that
time were expected to sacrifice themselves for the sake of their children
and their husbands. Norms about patriarchy and the dominance of males
over females abounded within the Church (O'Connor, 1998).

Inglis (2008) contends that most Irish women, during the 1950s and
1960s, willingly embraced Catholicism. 'The majority of Irish people gave
their hearts, minds and bodies to the Catholic Church. Catholic prayers
and rituals were at the heart of family life' (Inglis, 2008: 144) and 'the
family was at the heart of Irish social reproduction' (Inglis, 1998: 167).
Women gained status from being closely associated with the activities
of the local Catholic priests. Catholic teachings made sense of women's
lives of service to others, denial of self and prioritising of family needs
over individual needs. Women were assured that they would get their
reward in the 'next life', that is, after death, and that they should not
expect too much in this life. Women gained status from being responsible for producing the next generation of Catholics, many of whom were
expected to become priests and nuns. It was the height of respectability
and a source of family pride to have a daughter a nun or a son a priest
(Brody, 1974).

While there were benefits attached to Irish women's adherence to
Catholic doctrines and rules, there were also costs. One of these costs
involved having no access to artificial means of contraception. The papal
encyclical, *Humanae Vitae* 1967, which was issued as part of proceedings
at Vatican II, decreed that abortion, sterilisation and all artificial methods
of contraception were immoral. 'Similarly excluded is any action which
either before, at the moment of, or after sexual intercourse, is specifically
intended to prevent procreation—whether as an end or as a means' (Vatican,
1967:16). In the absence of contraception, Irish married women were con-
signed to having a large number of children. Within marriage, women
were expected to be sexually available for procreation (Hill, 2003). It was
the usual practice for women to seek advice on family planning or sexuality problems from the priest in the confessional (Ferriter, 2009) and not
from the doctor. Out of the fourteen women in the study, eleven of their

mothers had between four and nine children. Some also had a number of miscarriages or babies who died at birth.

One of the other costs for women of adherence to Catholic teachings was that they had no access to divorce and were expected to stay for life in marriages where there may have been serious difficulties, for example, alcohol abuse or domestic violence (O'Connor, 1998; Bacik, 2004). All of the women interviewed were adamant that separation was unthinkable in their families when they were growing up. The quotations presented in this chapter show the attitudes to separation that the women were aware of in their families, in their schools and in their churches when they were children. The women were aware of isolated cases of people who were separated (these were usually non-Irish or non-Catholic or living abroad) but they were embedded in the notion that separation was wrong for any members of their own families and they internalised this belief as children without even questioning it. They understood clearly that to separate would be to bring shame on themselves and on their family name. Identity and status came primarily from the family a person belonged to rather than attaching to the individuals themselves. A misdemeanour, for example a separation, by one member of the family would bring shame on the entire family and not just on the individual involved. Individual identity was subsumed under family identity. There was an inter-generational transfer of status and resources within families. Separation would involve a diminution of both status and resources and was to be avoided if at all possible.

The women understood, as children, that some people were unhappy in their marriages but the message they received from their parents was that it was not acceptable to leave an unhappy marriage. The right to individual happiness was not prioritised in Ireland at that time. The women also received the message that it was not appropriate to discuss marital separation. Silence, denial and shame surrounded the topic and the women, as children, did not think to question this view. To be separated was to be 'different', to be 'other' and 'not like us' and possibly 'no longer one of us'. Being separated was seen as posing a threat to the continuity of the family and possibly to the stability of society.

The women were deeply embedded in relationships with their families and with their communities, all of which, to a greater or lesser extent, espoused a Catholic conservative ethos where women and marriage were concerned. Except in very extreme circumstances, marital separation was not considered to be an option in the Ireland of the 1950s and early 1960s.

CHAPTER 3

Identity Formation in Young Adulthood

The women in this study reached young adulthood between the mid-1970s and early 1980s. In this chapter it is proposed to look at this stage of their lives, up to the point at which they got married. It is also proposed to continue to explore the first research question and to consider the relative importance into young adulthood of influence from families and communities. The concept of embeddedness is still very relevant. The concept of individualisation also becomes pertinent at this stage. The theory of individualisation will, firstly, be explained. Then data on leaving home and forming intimate relationships will be presented.

Individualisation

Individualisation, according to Giddens (2006), is a meta-concept which includes de-traditionalisation and the emergence of greater individual choice. According to this concept, there is a dis-embedding of social institutions. The argument is that individuals are increasingly free agents rather than being constrained by traditional structures such as the Church, social class or kinship networks. The theory suggests that, in modern society, the bonds between people and their families and between people and their religious groupings have been loosened and that what exists now is a society of individuals who freely form relationships with other individuals untrammelled by the constraints of tradition and in pursuit of individual fulfilment. However, '[a]s the traditions become progressively diluted, the promises of relationships grow' (Beck, 1992:113). Love is construed as the new centre around which people build their lives (Beck and Beck-Gernsheim, 1995) and the expectations of what loving the 'right' person can yield are very high.

Ideas on individualisation were largely developed in the USA, Germany and the UK, but elements of this thinking made their way to Ireland (largely through the media and through travel) and formed part of the backdrop, along with Catholic conservative ideology, to the Irish context in which the women in this study spent their late teenage years and early twenties.

Leaving Home

Seven of the sample went either to university or to teacher training college directly from school. One of these (Catherine) dropped out of college in order to get married at age twenty. Two of the women (Eileen and Irene) went abroad to work as au pairs, one to France and one to Belgium, before going on to train as nurses, one in Cork and one in London. The other women worked as secretaries, telephonists or shop assistants either in towns close to their homes or in Dublin. The practice of migrating from the country to Dublin in search of work or for study was common for young women at the time. Emigration was also common (Hill, 2003). Four of the fourteen women (Anne, Eileen, Irene and Mary) lived abroad for a number of years at different stages of their lives.

For some of the women, there was a sense of freedom and a desire for adventure in how they lived their lives as young adults. They were able to leave home and lead their own lives in their own way where previously they would have been under their parents' direction.

> IRENE: When I left school I came to Dublin. I worked in the Civil Service for a while, hated it. I did many jobs, worked as a waitress, worked as a barmaid, lots of things, trying to find what I wanted to do in life. Then I went to Brussels as an au pair for eighteen months, which I loved. But after eighteen months, I wanted to go

again so I went via London and I knew people in London who were doing nursing. I got an interview and I started nursing.

There is a sense of excitement and freedom about how Irene describes these years. She had grown up in rural Ireland, spent five years in boarding school and was ready for adventure. Anne was also ready for adventure but due to family illness had to cut her travels short.

> ANNE: I didn't really want to stay in Ireland. I wanted to spread my wings. I was dying to travel. One of my sisters had gone and of course I saw the good life she had. The first year after I qualified, I worked as a language assistant in France for a year. Then I didn't want to come home, so I came home for a while and I moved onto Spain then. I loved Spain. I loved learning Spanish. I was very happy there. I came home the following summer and my father got very sick, he had a stroke. So, I didn't go back after that. I felt, being the youngest I should stay at home and give them a hand out. I didn't really want to come home but I did. I felt they were getting elderly at this stage. Then, when I got the job here, I loved it. I settled in very well. I still love travel.

The impact of a parent's death and notions about family obligation and the female role in caring were common themes in the women's stories. Anne obviously felt a strong sense of obligation to return home to help take care of her father when he was ill, despite the fact that she had been enjoying life abroad. She also felt that because she was the youngest and still single (and female?) that she should be the one to help her mother when her father became ill.

For Kay, there was not quite the same sense of freedom or choice. She could leave home to complete her studies and to work but travel and buying her own house or apartment were out of the question.

> KAY: There was this assumption that you just get trained, get a job, get married. There was no talk of travelling or your own apartment!

Geraldine talked about feeling that she had no freedom as long as she lived with her parents. She lived in Dublin and stayed living with her parents until she got married.

GERALDINE: My parents were the sort of parents that if I was dating a boy, they would nearly call him aside on the second date and ask him what his intentions were. I felt I had absolutely no freedom to do anything and I just couldn't wait to get away.

Of the seven women who grew up in Dublin, six lived at home until they were married. The women from the country left home for work or to go to college so their lives as young adults were different than their counterparts from Dublin. They had greater freedom to create their own lifestyles but still within limits. They were expected to return home if they were needed and they were not expected to get mortgages or buy their own homes. That was to happen when they married. Marriage was part of the life-script to which young people were expected to aspire.

Forming Intimate Relationships

For all of the women, their courtships were a positive period in their lives and for many of them their relationships with their husbands-to-be were the first serious relationships that they experienced. Nine of the women had courtships that lasted between one and three years. The other courtships were even longer. Short courtships have been found (Clarke and Berrington, 1999) to lead to an increased risk of marriage breakdown. This was not the case for the women this study. Four of the women (Breda, Catherine, Jane and Kay) started going out with their prospective husbands when they were in their teens.

L: Tell me a bit about your courtship.
CATHERINE: Well I met Dennis when I was fifteen. I really wasn't an 'out and about' kind of person. I suppose for the first two years we were going out I met him on a Fri. night. I was only fifteen. But always around study time, doing my Junior/ Intermediate Cert and the Leaving Cert. I'd stop seeing him for about three months. We were very much together. He was very much a part of our family.

Kay started 'going out with' her husband-to-be when she was eighteen and he was twenty-two.

L: So how did you get on during this courtship?

KAY: We got on really well, really well. It was lovely, we had very similar interests. We were very interested in sport. We both liked the same kind of books. I regularly would go and buy a book for Brian and come home to find he'd bought the book for me. We enjoyed the same kind of things, he was very involved in the club here and I enjoyed going to it. We got on really well.

Irene, on the other hand, was slightly older and was living in London.

IRENE: George was younger than me. He was eighteen when I met him and I was just twenty. He was a lovely guy. He introduced me to a life I never knew really. He introduced me to music and literature and philosophy and paintings. We used to go to the galleries (in London). It was very exciting. I fell madly in love with this guy and he had great qualities. I mean he was very generous. He knew how to woo me. He came with the flowers and little gifts all the time. He was great fun, great company and I thought I was a very lucky person.

Mary and Frances similarly described getting on very well, spending lots of time together and having similar interests during their courtships.

MARY: Well from the minute we met we clicked, we always got on and we just always had a lot to talk about.

FRANCES: We went to the cinema. We went to plays. We went out for drinks. We went out for meals. We spent quite a lot of time together.

The picture that emerges from these quotations is of young people at the start of relationships who were very much in love and who were enjoying the new-found freedoms that young people in Ireland were beginning to enjoy in the Ireland of the late 1970s/early 1980s.

Pre-marital Sex

In some of the interviews, discussions about courtship led to discussions about pre-marital sex. Irene talked about her experiences of cohabiting prior to marriage. She lived in London with her husband-to-be (who happened to be English) for seven years before they married.

IRENE: We were able to live together because we were in London. I have a number of friends who got married when they were twenty one and they got married because they could not have a relationship in Ireland at the time. I felt free to do it, although my parents weren't aware of it. It just wasn't done. In fact, my sisters were disapproving of it.

L: Like if you came home to visit, you were talking separate bedrooms?

IRENE: Oh, absolutely. Even when I went on holidays, I used to send postcards home with my name and 'Georgina'. His name was never on the card.

L: It was that era where our generation were very different than our parents' generation. That shift had happened. Contraception had become available and we knew about it.

IRENE: Yes, and I was considered a little bit wild when I was young, although I wasn't wild as we know today. But I couldn't be told. I would do what I wanted to do.

L: You could do that more easily in England than you could in Ireland.

IRENE: Absolutely.

What I was alluding to here was that a change in attitudes and in legislation on contraception had occurred in Ireland. According to Ferriter (2009), unease about the ban on contraception had been growing in Ireland from the 1960s. In a landmark case in 1973, which later became known as 'the McGee case', it was argued that the special position of the family as enshrined in the Constitution meant that it was unconstitutional for the state to intrude in the privacy of the family. The case was won on that basis and the government was forced to begin to draft legislation on contraception.

In 1979 legislation on contraception was finally passed but contained seriously restrictive conditions. Contraceptives were only made available by doctor's prescription and from a pharmacist to *bona fide* married couples for family planning purposes. In order to overcome these restrictions, family planning clinics were set up, mainly by groups in the women's movement. Contraceptives were offered in return for cash donations, rather than for sale. Medical doctors were also free to prescribe the contraceptive pill as a menstrual cycle regulator for women. It was suggested that of the estimated 15,000 women in Ireland taking the contraceptive pill in 1968, 75% were taking it for non-medical reasons (Ferriter, 2009). As well as contraceptives being prescribed by doctors, they were also smuggled into the country so that, by a variety of means, many Irish people were beginning to gain access to artificial means of contraception (Tovey and Share, 2000; Ferriter, 2009).

The stories told by the women in this study clearly illustrate the fear, uncertainty and problems with access to family planning services that existed for young Irish adults prior to the 1980s.

Kay told stories about trying to buy contraceptives in the west of Ireland before she was married.

> KAY: We started dating, and I don't think he every actually asked me to marry him, it was assumed we would get married!
> L: Really, why?
> KAY: Because we were both very domestic kind of people, at the time.
> L: Anything to do with not having pre-marital sex?
> KAY: No, because we did. Yea, and I got a few frights doing it, and went in with pre-scriptions to chemists and was literally thrown out the door like a scarlet woman! And they were legal prescriptions, and literally 'we don't serve your kind here,' 'I remember sneaking along the quays to the family planning clinic to get a legal pre-scription! I was literally thrown out of two chemist shops publically! It was the most embarrassing, I couldn't believe it. I remember one particular nasty old man, he just threw it (the prescription) back and I had pick it up off the counter. 'We don't serve your kind here'.
> L: Because you weren't married?
> KAY: I think it was just the whole contraceptive thing. He just didn't stock the pill, full stop.

This pharmacist's attitude is indicative of the dominant conservative culture against artificial contraceptives that still prevailed, despite the fact that contraception had been legalised. Hill (2003) stated that a practice still persisted whereby people took it upon themselves to make a judgement on whether contraceptives should be used or not. She claims that despite contraception being legalised in 1979 that there was still ambivalence towards its use which resulted in information not being provided and contraceptives not being easily accessed by less educated and poorer sections of society.

Three of the women (Breda, Eileen and Jane) were pregnant getting married. Again, pre-marital pregnancy is linked in research (Clarke and Berrington, 1999) to increased risk of marriage breakdown. However, none of the three women felt it was a factor in their separations decades later. Jane was eighteen when she got married. She described herself as having been 'as green as the grass' when it came to knowing anything about contraception.

> L: You were pregnant getting married. Was that a big difficulty at the time?
> JANE: It was for me because my father came from kind of a well-respected family and my mother, her attitude was 'don't ever do anything to shame your father, don't ever', so the shame of me having to tell my father, but sure, they got over that.
> When we were there and we told my father and he said to John 'out the door'. He said, 'Just go' and John said 'No, I'm staying here'. So that said a lot for him at that stage, you know what I mean. So that was it, like, we just got on with it, like. Then we went to live with them actually for a while, and they were great support.

Women who became pregnant outside of marriage faced very difficult choices. They either had to get married very quickly in order to retain respectability (as the women in this study did), or they had to hide their pregnancies by going to Mother and Baby Homes and giving their babies up for adoption (Hill, 2003), or they had to go to England for abortions (Hill, 2003; Bacik, 2004). There was a clear taboo against single parenthood which made it almost impossible, culturally, financially and socially to raise a child outside marriage. It just was not done in 'respectable' families in Ireland at that time.

Mary presents a view on how unmarried motherhood was viewed in a poorer area, compared to how she felt it might be viewed in more middle class areas.

> MARY: See I grew up in inner city Dublin in a very poor area. Some of the young girls who would have been the same age as me, at about fifteen or sixteen, got pregnant 'accidentally on purpose' I would think, in order to get on the housing list. They didn't want to be married, they wanted to be an unmarried mother. Whereas maybe in a more middle class setting if you got pregnant your parent would have said 'Oh you have to get married straight away', whereas that wasn't the case there because they got higher up the social housing list by not being married.

Notions about class status and respectability as they relate to unmarried motherhood are echoed in these opinions. The case of Joanne Hayes, the woman who was at the centre of the 'Kerry Babies' case in 1983, provides a clear example of the attitudes that were in existence towards women who transgressed normative moral codes in Ireland in the 1980s. Joanne Hayes was a young woman who came from a farming background in County Kerry. She came from a 'well respected' family. She was having an affair with a married man and had a child with this man which she was raising in her family home. She became pregnant for a second time in 1983.

When two dead babies were found within the space of a fortnight in 1984 in County Kerry, Joanne, who was in her early twenties at that time, was accused of having given birth to twins and of having murdered them. In his account of the 'Kerry Babies Case', Inglis (2003) claims that 'to understand Joanne Hayes, it is necessary to understand the position of women in Irish society, how they were seen and understood and the stories that were told about them' (p. 8). The fact that such a story could be constructed and later defended in a tribunal was indicative of beliefs about 'loose' women who had children 'out of wedlock' and who had affairs with married men. The implication was that women who would behave in such an immoral fashion were also capable of murder and could be treated as murder suspects (Inglis, 2003).

In that type of climate, it is not surprising that fear of pregnancy during courtship was a common theme in the interviews for this study.

> MARY: Contraception was not available, I remember in UCD[1] they put a condom machine in the Students' Union and the authorities took it down because it was illegal so it wasn't like you could go into a chemist and buy something so that was my biggest fear. I was terrified I would get pregnant and it would ruin my life. That was my view. So I didn't sleep around or anything like that, so I guess in some way the social part of that did rub off on me.

Half of the women did not have sex before getting married.

> L: No sex before marriage?
> SARAH: No. That was the expectation and none of my friends; one girl I met in College did live with her boyfriend for a couple of months before they got married, and even I, at twenty-two, was kind of, God! You know, so there was no cohabiting at all.

---

1   University College Dublin.

L: There was no pressure,

SARAH: None at all.

L: To have sex.

SARAH: No, but then you see, we were just on the cusp of that stage, 'a gentleman wouldn't make advances to a lady', just nearly coming to ... I'd say within two years afterwards, it all changed.

Nora described getting advice from her mother when she was going out;

NORA: 'Mind herself'. We were never sure what we were to mind ourselves of ... You know you didn't ... A couple of week-ends I would have slept in the bed with Billy. But that was it. Do you know? That was it and he ... how could I put it ... he understood or he ... that was the way it was.

These excerpts clearly illustrate both the continuities and the changes that were taking place in how young women lived their lives and conducted their courtships in Ireland in the late 1970s/early 1980s. The *Unmarried Mother's Allowance* had been introduced in 1973 but there was still a stigma about unmarried motherhood and uncertainty about pre-marital sex (Hill, 2003; McCafferty, 2010). Cohabitation was very rare and usually hidden. There was still an expectation that couples would have a courtship for a few years before getting married and that children would be born within rather than outside marriage.

Hindsight on Some Early Warning Signs

In hindsight, some of the women could see early warning signs of the difficulties that were to come in their marriages but, at the time, they were enjoying the relationships and had no serious reservations about getting married.

L: When you look back on the courtship, what comes to mind?

ANNE: A lot of drinking

L: On his part?

ANNE: Yes. I do know that when we were going out, Noel was very good fun and he was a very kind person, I felt, at that stage, anyway. The thing was there was a lot of socialising in the pubs and I wasn't one for pubs but he was into music and played music and all that scene was in the pubs, I wasn't too fond of that really, but as it went along I suppose I just got used to it and I suppose I was pretty mad about him when we got married and I always wanted to get married too. It was a natural consequence for me, I felt.

L: So you were 29?

ANNE: Yes.

L: It was time for you?

ANNE: Yes, that's what I felt. When I think back, it (drink) was always really in the background. He did make promises that he would give it up but I wasn't strong enough. I didn't know he'd go back. I suppose because I was really mad about him at the time, I just stayed.

Deirdre tells a similar story, not about drink but about signs of anxiety and uncertainty about marriage on the part of her husband-to-be that she did not understand or appreciate the potential seriousness of at the time.

L: Is there anything about the courtship that you can remember, looking back, that caused you concern?

DEIRDRE: To me, Brendan had issues with commitment at the time. Between the time we got engaged and got married, he did at one stage say that he didn't want to get married. He suffered from anxiety and, probably, depression, even though at that time I wouldn't have had a clue that that's what it was. Had I been older, had I had more experience of life, I might have said 'hold on here, if he's not sure'. At twenty three and head over heels in love, there was no way anybody was going to tell me not to marry him. We had great fun together. We got on very well together. I was very happy.

Drink and depression are often linked with marital breakdown (McDonnell, 1999; McKeown *et al.*, 2004) but as young adults the women did not know enough about these conditions to see them as reasons not to get married.

Decision to Marry

It seemed to be a foregone conclusion, part of the cultural expectations and norms at the time that couples who were dating in their twenties would automatically proceed to marriage. Anne said earlier that she had always wanted to get married. Kay said that she never actually got a proposal of marriage. Her boyfriend quickly became included in activities by her siblings and her parents. It was just assumed that they would marry and have a family of their own.

> KAY: I think one of the reasons Brian may have been so keen to marry me at the time was he loved family and the security of my family.
> L: They welcomed him.
> KAY: They welcomed him and he just loved the whole idea of normality. My sisters and brothers were quite young and they loved him like an older brother and he played golf with my parents

Frances linked the timing of her decision to get married to her mother's death. The suddenness of the death shocked Frances into realising the importance of love in her life and into deciding to accept a proposal to get married.

> FRANCES: So I suppose I was left with a lot of time to think about things and my mother's death and the reality of life that you can have it all and then it can be gone so quickly and that it was about time, maybe, that I settled down and had my own children and stopped partying and got serious, because life was serious. For the first time in my life, life was serious. So I thought about it and I said 'yes'.

Getting married was about settling down and becoming 'serious' and there was an age by which that was supposed to happen. In the 1980s in Ireland the number of people getting married increased and the age at marriage decreased so that more young Irish people were getting married in their twenties (Kennedy, 2001).

Discussion: Individualisation during Young Adulthood

From the 1960s and 1970s onwards the influence of the Catholic Church began to wane (O'Connor, 1998). There had been a move away from agriculture and an opening up of the economy and the society to more liberal influences from outside the country. Irish television stations (RTE) had begun broadcasting in 1961. Young people moved in search of employment to towns and cities away from the traditional and conservative attitudes that were prevalent in rural areas. This afforded greater freedom from the influence of extended families and local communities.

The 1980s in Ireland were described as a time when 'young people were caught between remaining loyal to the Catholic vision and interpretation of life, and breaking free and creating a new meaning and identity' (Inglis, 2003:9). Young women were torn between embeddedness in conservative beliefs about gender, sex and marriage and liberal 'individualised' beliefs about the right to individual freedom and choice. It is generally acknowledged (Hill, 2003; Bacik, 2004; Ferriter, 2009) that the sexual revolution which happened in other countries in the sixties did not really come to Ireland until the eighties. The excerpts on pre-marital sex in which over half the women indicated that they were afraid to use contraceptives or to engage in pre-marital sex illustrate that sex outside marriage was still not the norm in Ireland in the 1980s but that change was beginning to happen. The difficulties encountered by the Government in passing contraception legislation show the type of conservative attitudes that were still dominant in Ireland at this time.

Yet, some liberal views were beginning to be voiced. The second wave of the women's movement in the 1970s in Ireland had shifted many of the accepted essentialist assumptions about women in Irish society. Entry to the EU (EEC)[2] in 1973 had resulted in a raft of equality legislation being introduced (O'Connor, 1998; Hill, 2003; Ferriter, 2004). Irish television broadcasting had an impact by making different images of women available, other than those presented by the Church. Foreign programmes challenged the natural inevitability in women's roles in families and in society (O'Connor, 1998).

The excerpts show some of the women's abilities to 'pick and mix' between the traditional Catholic practices they had grown up with and the more liberal modern options they were exposed to as young adults. For example, by buying contraceptives in a town in which they were not known (Kay) or by cohabiting in England (Irene) where they could not

2   European Union, formerly called the European Economic Community.

be seen by parents or by disapproving older siblings, they were breaking the rule on pre-marital sex but in a manner that would not subject them to censure. They appeared to be overtly staying within the rules of society and at the same time they managed to have a degree of individual freedom.

The statements of the women reflect evidence of increasing individualisation in how some of them were able to live their own lives once they left home. Their stories reflect the growing levels of freedom to develop individual identities that some of the women displayed during their young adulthood. They show that life chances and choices were no longer so fully determined by family status. Several of the women followed individual agendas and left Ireland in search of freedom and adventure. Some of them engaged in pre-marital sex and used artificial methods of contraception. They could have 'a bit of a life of their own' (Beck and Beck-Gernsheim, 2002:55) in Dublin or in London. However, the women remained connected to their families of origin and all of them eventually returned to settle, that is to marry and to raise children, in Ireland. Marriage based on love or a 'pure relationship' (Giddens, 1992) was still seen as the 'ideal' situation for a woman. None of the women wanted to be 'left on the shelf' or to be 'spinsters' and they did not question the reality behind the ideal of lifelong marriage based on love. Even where there were signs of problems with alcohol and mental health, these were not picked up on in the headlong rush to be married and be the same as everyone else in their age cohort in Ireland.

CHAPTER 4

Experiences during Marriage: Practical Aspects

The volume of data on the women's experiences during marriage was such that two chapters are devoted to this period of their lives. This chapter deals with the practical aspects and the following chapter deals with the more emotional and relational aspects. The second research question about the processes and events that led to the women's separations is addressed. The concepts which underpin much of the discussion are the concepts of love and care. These concepts will be explained before presenting the data on the women's experiences of raising children, their satisfaction with the division of household tasks and the impact of work and money difficulties on their relationships.

Love and Care

The concept of love on its own was considered to be problematic because its meaning is so contested and it is so often just equated with romantic or passionate love. 'Intimacy' was considered but rejected because it tends to be associated primarily with sexual relations. The concept of 'love labour' was used in the original dissertation. It was used because the two words 'love' (or the absence of love) and 'labour', meaning the work needed to sustain a relationship, are such key concepts in understanding the data on marriage and marriage difficulties. Feedback from readers of earlier drafts indicated that the phrase 'love labour' was awkward and they disliked the word 'labour' being used in the same phrase as 'love' to describe marriage.

'Care' was inserted in place of 'labour'. According to Fisher and Tronto (1990), care has four phases which are linked to four moral values. It involves 'caring about' a person and being attentive to their needs. It means 'caring for' a person and feeling responsible for their well-being. It entails 'taking care' of a person and being competent at providing care. It includes 'care-receiving' and showing responsiveness to the care that is provided. The two concepts, 'love and care', taken together capture not just the declaration of love and the feeling of being loved but also the activities that are associated with showing love and care on a daily basis.

Love and care involve being other-centred rather than self-centred. They operate at a number of different levels. At a practical level, showing love and care entails, for example, going out to work to earn money for a family, doing household tasks, taking care of children, cooking favourite meals, shopping with the other's preferences in mind and keeping house with an eye to the other's comfort. At a mental level, being loving and caring involves keeping the other in mind, prioritising their needs and interests and planning around the other. At a cognitive level, love and care involve understanding and being 'tuned' into the other. At an emotional level, love and care's principal goal is the well-being of the other (Lynch, 2007: 557). Love changes the meaning of everyday activities (Smart, 2007), resulting in activities being interpreted as signs of love or as signs of the absence of love. Patterns of showing love or of not showing love emerge in how marital and parental relationships are conducted. These patterns can engender greater connectedness and greater intimacy or they can lead to increasing disconnectedness and fragmentation. Love and care require time and commitment into the future, 'til death do us part', within a marital relationship.

Being loving and caring involves management of the tensions and conflict which are an integral part of all relationships. They involve caring enough about the other person to make a concerted effort to resolve arguments. They involve being assertive enough to say the things that need to be said in a manner that respects the other person. They involve being prepared to listen, accept and act on what is being said in a constructive manner (McKeown et al., 2003).

Profiles of Women during Marriage

Table 2 shows that the women's courtships typically lasted between two and three years, the shortest being twelve months and the longest being seven years (for the couple who were living together abroad). Marriages took place between 1978 and 1987. The women were mostly in their mid-twenties when they got married. Twelve of the fourteen women had Church weddings. The remaining two (Breda and Mary) got married in registry offices, one in Ireland and one in the US. All of the women went on to have children. Just one woman (Mary) had a single child. Eight of the fourteen women had three children. The remaining five women had two children. Three of the women were pregnant getting married. These profiles mirror the patterns of family formation that were common in Ireland in the 1980s in terms of the age at marriage and the size of families (Fahey and Field, 2008).

Table 2: Profiles of the Women during Marriage

Name	Length of Courtship	Year Married	Age at Marriage	Number of Children	Woman's Occupation (Previous)	Year of Separation
Anne	30 months	1987	29 (f) 31 (m)	2	Professional	2008
Breda	18 months	1978	20 21	2	Carer (Housewife)	2003
Catherine	5 years	1974	20 23	3	Professional	2009
Deirdre	30 months	1978	23 30	2	Professional	2005
Eileen	20 months	1983	29 28	3	Professional	2009
Frances	30 months	1982	25 31	3	Professional	2005
Geraldine	20 months	1985	24 24	3	Clerical	2005

Name	Length of Courtship	Year Married	Age at Marriage	Number of Children	Woman's Occupation (Previous)	Year of Separation
Helen	6 years	1984	23 24	3	p/t Clerical (Housewife)	2006
Irene	7 years	1982	27 25	3	Professional	2008
Jane	18 months	1982	18 18	3	p/t shop Assistant (Housewife)	2008
Kay	12 months	1982	21 23	2	Professional	2004
Sarah	3 years	1981	28 31	3	Professional	2006
Mary	5 years	1986	25 26	1	Former business exec. returning to education	2008
Nora	2 years	1980	23 24	2	p/t shop Assistant (Housewife)	2009

Note: The interviews were conducted in July and August 2010.

The women's occupations also mirrored the type of occupations in which women in Ireland were typically employed (Hill, 2003). Those with third-level education worked in education and health. Those with second-level education worked in clerical or secretarial positions. Those who had less education leaving school tended to work part-time in shops or in the service sector. In Table 2 it was not possible to capture the variety of full and part-time jobs that the women held during their marriages. The insertion of housewife in brackets indicates that for much of these four women's (Breda, Helen, Jane and Nora) married lives their principal occupation was that of full-time housewife. It was also not possible to show the stages at which many of the women had studied for degrees either during their marriages or during their separations. By the time the interviews were conducted in the summer of 2010, thirteen of the fourteen women had obtained Degree (11) and Masters (2) level qualifications.

The proportion of this group of women who are employed as professionals and who have third-level qualifications marks them out as being a predominantly middle class group of women. That most of the women were in employment also marks them out as being somewhat different to a substantial minority of women in Ireland. Recent statistics show that the rate for female employment was 56.4% in 2010 (CSO, 2011). Previous studies (Lunn *et al.*, 2009; Moore, 2010) have shown that single and separated women have a higher employment rate than married women.

Transition to Parenthood

Becoming parents for the first time has been identified by Carter and McGoldrick (2005) as the most difficult transition in the family life-cycle. It involves what Bateson (1989) terms 'an entire restructuring of life around commitments to others' (p. 75). Lunn *et al.* (2009), in their analysis of census trends in Ireland between 1986 and 2006, identified that the risk of marital breakdown increased by 25 to 30 percent for couples with one child compared to those with no children or those with two children. Their 'favoured explanation is that a first child can put a strain on a relationship, while having more children is a sign that any strains have been overcome' (p.x). Analysis of the data for this study echoes the sentiment that a first child can put a strain on a relationship but would not support the view that having a second child indicates that relationship issues have been overcome, as couples with two and three children went on to separate in this study.

Difficult Transition

More than half of the women described how difficult life became when their first child entered their lives. Three of them (Deirdre, Mary and Geraldine) traced the beginnings of the subsequent problems in their marriages to the trouble they experienced in becoming parents for the first time. Deirdre described how difficult life was in the first few months and years of her baby's life.

> DEIRDRE: I suppose, things changed very much when we had our first child.
> L: How did they change?
> DEIRDRE: They changed because there was so much more to do. Our first child was a very difficult baby. He was sick with ear infections from the time he was three months old until he was about seven. I'd say we didn't get our first full night's sleep until he was about two or two and a half and the strain that that put on us both as individuals and as a couple ... I would often say that was the beginning of the end ...

Mary, who had a child after nine years of marriage, clearly linked the difficulties in her marriage to how she and her husband coped with having their daughter. They were living abroad and had no family support. As they were both working in full-time, pressurised jobs, they took turns at getting up at night with the child. Mary described the birth of her daughter as follows;

> MARY: And we had our daughter. It was great and it was terrible at the same time. We were both scared. No family there, no nothing, and I remember after she was born and I'm sitting there feeding her every few hours feeling like a milk cow and she was a bit colicky in the evenings and I remember calling Pat saying 'you have to come home now she won't stop crying' because I'm there on my own with her. She [her infant daughter] would wake up six times a night. Three years of sleep deprivation took its toll. We never got back on an even keel.

Geraldine also described the birth of her first child as a shock and how she too was unable to cope with sleepless nights at the same time as holding down a full-time job.

> GERALDINE: In particular, the first one, he was born out of love and it was such a shock to my system, the responsibility of it. I think I must have had a bit of post-natal depression but I didn't see that. I didn't tell anybody, even the nurse that came in and I was breast feeding and I couldn't feed the child. He was only starving, the poor child. I just found it very stressful and I couldn't bring myself to getting up during the night and Tom ended up having to do that. He couldn't handle my emotional distress at all. He didn't know what to do with it but the way he handled it was he looked after the child. He was the one that walked the boards at night. I couldn't hack it. He has always held that against me.

The expectation in the above extract seems to be that it was the norm for a woman to be able to cope with a new baby and a job, and that a woman who could not cope had to hide her distress and felt, in some way, judged as being deficient and not measuring up to how an ideal mother was supposed to behave. There seems to have been very little understanding of post-natal depression. Rather than feeling supported by her husband taking on the night shift with a crying baby, Geraldine felt judged and found wanting.

A number of the women mentioned, in hindsight, that they probably had post-natal depression but they did not name it as such at the time. That Geraldine did not feel she could admit to being so stressed and unable to cope with her new baby, and that she and her husband were unable to communicate about her distress may be indicative of her fearing that she was failing in a task which society presents as always being a 'happy event' and as being 'natural' for a mother. Carter and McGoldrick (2005) suggest that the transition to parenthood can be the most difficult transition in the life course, but that it is often idealised by society. Bateson (2000) states that in many societies there are no expectations that a woman would be able to take care of her first or possibly, second or third child, on her own. She describes practices where the first time mother's mother and sisters are on hand to take care of the child for a number of years and questions the expectations in Western society that couples (mothers, in particular) should be able to cope alone, at the same time as being expected to have full-time jobs.

Geraldine and her husband went on to have two more children. The second child was a 'dream baby'. The third child was not sick but 'he didn't sleep for two and a half years'. Tom 'absented himself from night duty from the second child on, just like that.' Again it would appear that there was no discussion between the couple about who was going to care for the second baby. For the birth of the third child 'he sat in the corner doing the cross-word and keeping an eye on the game whereas the first time he was there holding my hand and they had to tell him to get out of the way' (Geraldine).

Not feeling connected, not being able to communicate about emotionally difficult topics and not feeling supported at times of need are examples of the type of disconnection in relationships that emerged as recurring themes throughout the interviews. In the 1980s in Ireland, when these women were having their babies, maternity leave consisted of fourteen weeks with pay and four weeks without pay. The experiences described above raise questions about the adequacy of the State support provided at that time for families with new babies in Ireland. If support from extended family was not available, usually in the form of a mother or a sister, then it appears that new parents were expected to cope on their own.

Not-So-Difficult Transition

Other women told very different stories about how they and their husbands coped with childbirth, illness and sleepless nights. They described care and love being shown by both partners in a variety of ways. When describing the birth of her first son, Irene said;

> IRENE: My first son was born when I was thirty and that was a very exciting time. We did natural child birth together. George came to all the classes. He was so supportive. I loved being pregnant. I had lovely clothes. I just loved the whole thing. It was a very, very exciting time for us. George came to the birth and was really, really supportive. I was sick, really, because I got septicaemia in labour but he was great, he really was.

Her husband was equally involved in the birth of the second child and he actually helped to deliver the third child when she arrived unexpectedly at home. Irene's babies were not easy to take care of or healthy all the time. The first child was 'forever sick' and the second child was 'a tear-away' but these were not described as issues that lead to difficulties in the couple's relationship.

Frances tells similar stories about her transition to parenthood.

> FRANCES: We went out a lot and my neighbour used to laugh, 'wait 'til that baby is born. That'll change your life.' When you're pregnant on your first baby, you don't know the changes that are going to be in your life. But I was happy. I was ready for a baby and Sean was very good with children. He was excellent, I have to say. He was just a big child himself.

There was a sense, for some of these mothers, that raising the children was a joint project in which both parents shared and in which they supported each other. They shared the job of caring for and raising their children. The transition to parenthood was experienced as a transition that could be tackled together.

Other mothers and fathers adopted more traditionally gendered roles, with the mothers (Breda, Jane, Helen) doing the majority of the childcare and the fathers going out to work. This was not a problem where the women also held traditional views on their roles.

The experiences described above demonstrate that the manner in which couples coped with child-bearing and child rearing show significant differences. Some parents coped very well with sleepless nights and sick children. Others found that the stress involved put a strain on their relationships. Not feeling supported by their partners, not being able to talk honestly about their concerns, not having their worries taken seriously and not feeling loved or cared for emerged as common themes in examples given of relationships which were deteriorating.

Satisfaction with the Division of Household Tasks

The division of household tasks was linked very closely in the women's stories to discussions about the tasks involved in caring for children. Nine of the fourteen women worked in full-time employment throughout their married lives. Twelve of the fourteen women had described their own mothers as full-time housewives so seven of these nine women were the first generation of mothers in their families to have worked full-time outside the home. Some of these women tried to combine full-time work with doing everything for their children. This was the model of motherhood with which they had grown up.

> ANNE: I was looking after him and the home and all the rest, I had also given an awful lot to my children. I felt nobody could do things for my children only me when they were young. Now I know that is not the right thing to do but then I felt that. I had a lot of toing and froing with the children. All that responsibility was mine, dropping them, picking them up, bringing them to whatever.

Five of the women spent periods at home full-time, interspersed with working in part-time positions which fitted in around their children's school times.

> JANE: It fitted and I was always here then. It finished at 12 o'clock and I was home, and you know I was in the yard, where they were, I was in the school where they were going to school and if ever there was a problem I was there, you know.

Recent research carried out in the U.K. (Sigle-Rushton, 2010) found that divorce rates were lower in families where husbands shared housework, shopping and childcare. 'A study of 3,500 British married couples after the birth of their first child found that the more the men helped, the lower the incidence of divorce'. The correlation is not that clear in the data for this study.

Several of the husbands did their share of cooking and cleaning.

> EILEEN: David always tidied up and would have done house work. If he came in the door at six o'clock, having been gone to work for ten hours, and I was feeding a child, he just went ahead and got the dinner and then went out and did his farming. You never had to ask him to do anything. If he saw clothes, he would put them in the washing machine and then when the washing machine was finished, he would hang them out.

> NORA: Whoever was home first cooked the dinner. Billy mightn't have been the greatest at hoovering or tidying up, but he'd put on or he'd hang out a wash. He'd tidy, he'd wash the dishes. He never expected his dinner on the table when he came home. As I said, whoever was home first would do the dinner. If I was working late he'd cook the dinner, so he did help out around the house.

There were also stories about men who had helped out with housework initially but who stopped as the years passed.

> DEIRDRE: As the children got that bit older, Brendan wasn't doing his share of work in the house. When Jenny was a baby, I decided to get someone to come into the house. I often say that those four years were the happiest, the least stressful, four years that I had. I came home every evening to a tidy house and things were fine then. I suppose when my youngest started school, a whole new set of problems arose. There was always housework and all this had to be done now and I was the one that was doing it. Basically Brendan came in from work at half six in the evening and his

dinner was on the table and he went from there to a chair to watch the news and read the paper. No matter how often I tried to explain to him how difficult it was to be working a whole day and then coming home to all this, it didn't seem to sink in.

In some cases, the connectedness which had been present at the start of marriages weakened over time and the division of household tasks and childcare became more traditional. This is a common trend found in research (Carter and McGoldrick, 2005), that many marriages revert to more traditionally gendered roles during the child-rearing years.

Where couples had a very traditional division of tasks, it did not seem to be an issue for some of the women that their husbands did so little housework during the course of their marriages. Breen and Cooke (2005) found that 23% of Irish married females and 31% of Irish married males could be classified as 'traditional' types. The crucial factor seems to be whether both parties were happy about how household tasks were shared and whether they felt loved or cared for rather than whether they actually did equal shares of the work (McKeown *et al.*, 2004).

> JANE: I did everything! Presents, birthdays, everything, his clothes, everything. Communions, Confirmations, Christmas ... John wouldn't know what Santa would be after bringing them until we would be putting them together that night. He supplied the money, end of story. He'd come home and he'd do the garden, or he'd wash the cars. No, like I really thought we had the balance right. I was as happy as Larry in my own home, with the three girls.

Both Helen and Jane stated that they wanted to be at home full-time with their children. They found it less stressful than trying to juggle work, childcare and running a home

> HELEN: I didn't want to stay on at work. Because Jim considered his job to be more important than my job, he wouldn't be willing to take time off if they were sick or anything like that. When the eldest girl was small and I was at work, if anything came up, it was always me that had to take time off. I could see the pattern. I couldn't cope with that kind of stress and I wanted to be at home.

It is only in retrospect, after having discovered infidelity, in particular, that many of the women were angry and resentful at the amount of work they did that was unseen and taken for granted. Both Helen and Jane stated that they thoroughly enjoyed being at home full-time with their children and that it is only now, following separation, that they realise how vulnerable not having an income and a career outside the home has left them.

There were also accounts in which women were seriously upset during their marriages by how little housework their husbands did and where they made a clear connection between their resentment over being left to do all the work and the deterioration of their relationships. The meaning the women attached to their husband's behaviour ('if he loved me, he would help me') in not sharing the household tasks was what caused the trouble and this meaning was not communicated to the men in a manner which led to a change in their behaviour. McKeown *et al.* (2004) describe this type of encounter as an example of a demand-withdrawal dynamic, whereby the woman asks for/ 'nags'/demands help, the man hears her request as criticism and instead of changing his behaviour, he withdraws, which she then reads as further evidence that he does not love her and she withdraws. Examples of this pattern of interaction will be shown over and over in the quotations that follow.

> KAY: Brian would be gone, as I said he was involved with a club. I had just had the first baby and I was sitting here at home, trying to get everything done and he might not arrive home until 10 or 11 at night. I remember one time when my daughter was taken in for tonsillitis and he was left at home with my son and he did nothing all weekend, and when I came home Monday and had been told not to leave the house with my daughter for two days, and discovered there wasn't even milk in the house. It hadn't occurred to him, and I just couldn't get it across to him. I found that really odd even at the time. He just didn't see that he had the time to do these things, even though I could see he had just watched sport or whatever. He always had the idea that he would help but it was always 'help', it wasn't his responsibility. That irritated me more and more as time went on.

Breda has a child with special needs and found the fact that her husband was 'very traditional' and that she was getting 'no hands-on help' to be a significant factor in her decision to separate. Her husband was not helping with all the additional work entailed in having a child with special needs and Breda was not able to explain how much this hurt her.

BREDA: It's not so much what was said or done, but what all that was unsaid and undone. 'If you're not happy, you know where the door is'. Gerry actually said that to me. I just wanted him to meet me half way. Instead of saying how really angry that made me, I just choked.

There are elements of patriarchal thinking evident in some of the quotations. Helen's statement that her husband always considered his job as being more important than hers is one example. Kay's perception that her husband felt that childcare and domestic tasks were primarily her responsibility, with which he would occasionally help, is another example of traditional gender-role thinking. These are just two examples amongst many the women gave of how embedded they felt their husbands were in traditional expectations of what constituted women's work and men's work.

Financial Problems

Many men define themselves in terms of their jobs and feel that working is their way of providing for and showing love to their wives and children. It does not appear from the data below that the opposite would be the case, in other words, that a man who did not go out to work would be seen as not showing love and care to his wife and children. However, in seven out of the fourteen cases, the women linked their separations to problems relating to the men's work or lack of work. In the following case, the man had frequent job changes or periods of unemployment and he could not seem to get settled in one job.

HELEN: Jim kept changing jobs and moving around. If he didn't like the way stuff was going in a job, he would just leave it and get somewhere else. I wasn't happy about that because of continuity and all of that. He would never discuss it. That was his thing. It was part of him and it had nothing to do with me.

As in the earlier discussions about the sharing of childcare and household tasks, it was not the problems in work *per se* that caused the problems in the marriage but how the couples communicated or failed to communicate that was the issue.

CATHERINE: But Dennis was having difficulty in work at that time. He finds it very difficult to express his feelings. He finds it very difficult to tell you he is troubled but he did tell me he was going to see someone around stress and work. It was clearly just to see how he would manage his work situation. Somewhere along the line a mutual friend of ours said to me 'Catherine, is Dennis out of work?' I said 'no' but I never asked him.

L: Did he get up every morning like he was going to work?

CATHERINE: Yes and I never asked him.

Three of the men set up their own businesses which failed, resulting in them amassing debts. Financial insecurity was an issue in these instances. Rows over money became a feature of relationships. The women got tired of paying all the bills and feeling like the responsible ones in the relationships, while their husbands took no responsibility.

FRANCES: Sean brought an unfair dismissals case against work which meant that he was off. I can't remember how long.

L: How upset was he through that whole process?

FRANCES: Well you see this is it. He never actually verbalised that to me. Then he started up his own business and it just didn't work out. He had pumped a lot of money into that, thinking 'this is going to go somewhere'. Friends had helped him out as well so they were business people and they could see that it was a good idea. As far as I was concerned, there really wasn't any choice but to go down this road anyway. So that's the road he went down and it just didn't work out.

L: Were you in debt?

FRANCES: Oh, huge, huge and that's when I became very terrified about how I would spend my life. There were bills coming in the door. Everything was in chaos, bills-wise. The bills were mounting up on the hall table until there were about sixty letters and he wouldn't open them. He just never bothered.

Irene's husband was self-employed and she was a manager. She described how she covered almost all of the household expenses.

IRENE: George never earned over ten thousand euro a year. I probably was earning sixty thousand a year, but it was all committed, I paid health insurance, I paid the mortgage, I paid life insurance, there were so many commitments, but it was all very much for our future together.

At no point was she considering separating from her husband just because he did not have a steady income. She stated that she 'loved the guy' and just wanted him to be a bit more responsible. She described the day she finally insisted that he pay some of the bills;

> IRENE: There was a time I went away on a three week holiday with my sisters a few years back and when I got back, they had had a fantastic time, George and the kids. He had done some work and got paid for some of the work. But when I got back, the bills were on the table waiting for me. So I thought 'this is crazy. I'm not taking this anymore'. So I said to him 'there may be bills on the table, but from this day forward they are your bills. I am not paying for everything'. Things started to go pear-shaped at that stage.

In other cases there were differences between the partners about how money was to be spent. Eileen gave up her job once she got married so she no longer had her own income. Sarah continued to work but she moved into a house which her husband had bought before they got married. Decisions about how money should be spent caused problems in both relationships.

> EILEEN: I had lived with having my salary and I had had my various accounts, a loan for my car and whatnot but I knew once I got married that I didn't have anything. It was a huge bone of contention from the point of view that David would say 'we haven't got the money', even though he had a reasonable salary at the time and we didn't have a mortgage. The control, the expectation for me to just be in that house and go no further than the local town and just not be able to be spontaneous and say 'we'll go off to another town today and we'll do this' ... That was very much frowned upon. I wasn't really meant to do that.

> SARAH: If I wanted to change the wallpaper in the bedroom 'sure it's grand! Why would you want to change that?' When the carpets were manky 'sure they're fine!' In other words there are no holes in them yet. He'd head straight over to the remnants bucket to buy the cheapest paper that he would like. And I'd say but look at the ... and then again he'd kind of insinuate that I was from an indulgent family, 'that's the way you were reared' and it wasn't nice.

In the cases where financial insecurity was a problem and where men were having trouble in work, many of the men were unable to discuss their problems with their wives. Several of the wives seem to have been supportive of whatever decisions their husbands made about their careers, but a pattern of regular job changes and failed business ventures took their toll on family finances and on relationships. There seems to have been a sense whereby the women felt that the men were leaving all the responsibility for managing the family finances to them. They saw it as another example of the men not helping them and not sharing the work of managing the family. They felt over-burdened, unsupported and unloved. In other cases, women felt that the men wanted to control all decisions about how money was spent and that this was symptomatic of control generally within their relationships. In both scenarios the problem was a mismatch of expectations and an inability to communicate about the differences in a manner that led to satisfactory compromises for both parties.

Discussion: Problems with Love and Care in Marriage

Structural changes in society, difficulties in interpersonal relationships and difficulties in individual personalities are most often cited in literature as the 'causes' of marriage breakdown (Smart, 1999; Wolcott and Hughes, 1999; Amato, 2000; Lowenstein, 2007). As this book is being written primarily from a sociological perspective, problems related to individual personalities are beyond the scope of this study. Broader structural changes, such as increasing individualisation and secularisation, women's employment outside the home and changing attitudes to gender equality form the backdrop to the marriages and to the problems that emerged in the marital relationships of the fourteen women in this study.

Prior to the 1960s and 1970s, economic considerations, often relating to property and land rather than romantic love, were considered to be the most important aspects to take into account when choosing a marriage partner. Men and women lived in very separate worlds. Men went out to work. Women stayed at home to mind the children. The traditional male breadwinner model was the norm. From the 1960s onwards, relationships based on love and equality began to be seen as essential for marriage (O'Connor, 1998).

There is evidence in the narratives in this chapter to suggest that most of the women expected their husbands to share the childcare and housework, especially in situations where both parents were working. Many of the men shared this expectation. As the quotations from Eileen and Nora show, these men did not expect their wives to do all the housework and childcare and were happy to share the work equally. Where this was the case, the transition to parenting and the division of household tasks were not the issues which led to eventual separation.

Other couples (Jane and Helen) adopted very traditional roles in relation to childcare and the division of household tasks. The women were happy to care for the children and to do all the housework. The men went to work and took care of the garden, the car and the house maintenance. These couples were embedded in traditional gender roles and both parties were happy to play traditional roles.

For some dual-earning couples (Geraldine and Mary), it was not that the men did not share in the childcare but that, as a consequence of both parents caring for the child as well as having full-time jobs, they did not have the time or the energy to put the work into caring for each other. They became disconnected from each other due to the pressure of trying to manage so many responsibilities.

However, for other couples (Kay and Breda) there was a clear mismatch in expectations about responsibility for childcare and housework. Breda stated that the key factor in her decision to separate was that her husband would not 'meet her half-way' in helping to care for her daughter who has special needs. He did not share the work of caring for their daughter and his wife saw this as a sign, not only that he did not love his daughter sufficiently but also, that he did not love her. In these cases, it was not just the mismatch in expectations about the 'doing' of love and showing care that was the problem. There was also a problem in not being able to arrive at a solution.

McDonnell (1999) put forward a thesis that 'marital breakdown and separation are in essence a failure on the part of the couple to negotiate mutually acceptable roles within the marriage' (p. 118). Kay said she could not get her husband to understand why she was upset that he did not take responsibility for doing housework. Breda blamed herself for not being assertive enough in explaining why she needed her husband to help. She felt she could have strengthened their relationship by discussing with her husband how they both felt about having a child with special needs.

The women were unable to bridge the gap in perspective between their husbands and themselves. They were unable to establish roles with which they were both happy. It was as if the men and the women were still living in separate spheres, as they had done in their parents' generation, but that the women were no longer content with that arrangement. Couples were playing old established roles, those of father and mother, husband and wife, but the women wanted to play the old roles by new, more egalitarian rules (Carter and McGoldrick, 2005). Some of the men did appear to not understand what was expected of them under the new 'rules' and the women seem to have been unable to explain what they needed or wanted the men to do. A mismatch in expectations and a gap in communications resulted in relationships becoming strained over time.

CHAPTER 5

Experiences during Marriage:
Relational and Emotional Aspects

There are numerous areas of overlap between the two chapters on the women's experiences during marriage. The practical aspects of marriage already discussed have clearly got emotional and relational consequences. This chapter includes some socio-psychological literature (Duck, 1998: Aronson *et al.*, 2003) on the phases and typical behaviours that occur in the breakdown of relationships. Data are presented on the overall quality of the women's relationships with their spouses, the nature of sexual relations, methods of resolving conflict, significant turning points in marriages, awareness of the gradual deterioration of relationships and attendance at marriage counselling.

Phases of Dissolving Personal Relationships

Aronson *et al.* (2003) present a range of theories which are useful when analysing the manner in which intimate relationships are terminated. Two of those theories are outlined here; Duck (1998) and Rusbult (1996). Duck (1998:89) suggests that there are four main phases in the process of dissolving personal relationships: intra-physic phase, dyadic phase, social phase and grave dressing phase. He also stated that each phase is accompanied by a threshold phrase: 'I can't stand this anymore', 'I'd be justified in withdrawing', 'I mean it' and 'it's now inevitable' (p. 89). The first phase is an intra-psychic phase during which a person who is dissatisfied starts thinking about the negative aspects of the relationship, assesses the adequacy of their partner's behaviour and considers the cost of withdrawal. This is followed by a dyadic phase during which the person is faced with the 'confrontation/avoidance dilemma' (p. 89). They may try to talk about the difficulties with their partner and attempt repair and reconciliation. If efforts at reconciliation fail, Duck (1998) contends relationships are ended and couples engage in a social phase which involves 'negotiating a post-dissolution state with a partner, creating face-saving/blame-placing stories and accounts and considering and facing up to implied social network effects' (p. 89). The final phase, what Duck calls the 'Grave Dressing Phase', entails 'getting over' the break-up and engaging in retrospection, attribution and 'public distribution of their own version of the break-up story' (p. 89).

Elements of the intra-physic phase were apparent in the previous chapter in which some of the women described their dissatisfaction with their husbands' lack of involvement in household and childcare tasks, as well as their unease at their husbands' poor employment records or financial management skills. During this phase, Duck (1998) found that it is a common practice not to disclose the strains in a marital relationship to anyone. This was the case with the women in this study. They endured years of unhappiness in isolation.

Examples of the dyadic phase are found in this chapter which details increased awareness of deteriorating relationships, attempts to resolve the problems, consideration of separation and attendance at counselling. This dyadic phase was not experienced by all of the couples. As will be seen in later descriptions of cases of infidelity, partners who were having affairs would appear to have opted for avoidance rather than confrontation. These last two phases are relevant for the later chapters which outline the events and processes that occurred at the time of separation and the activities partners engaged in during the post-separation phase.

The Exit-Voice-Loyalty-Neglect Typology

Another useful typology presented by Aronson *et al.* (2003: 375) is adapted from Rusbult *et al.* (1996). It builds on social exchange theory to construct an investment model comprised of four types of behaviour that occur in troubled relationships. Active behaviours can be either constructive or destructive. Active behaviours which are destructive lead to *exit* from a relationship. Active behaviours which are constructive consist of people voicing their concerns and engaging in dialogue/*voicing* about them. Passive behaviours can also be either constructive or destructive. Passive behaviours which are destructive constitute acts of omission or behaviours which *neglect* to actively support caring relationships. Passive behaviours which are constructive are motivated by *loyalty* to the other person, to children, to extended family or to the institution of marriage.

Many of the behaviours described during the women's twenty years of marriage fit into the neglect, voice and loyalty quadrants. Some of the women felt neglected or unappreciated by their husbands but blamed themselves for neglecting to confront the issues at an early stage. They were showing loyalty to their husbands, their children and extended families by waiting and hoping that relationships would improve. They eventually gave voice to their concerns by going to counselling, either as couples or individually. The exit piece was the next phase and is the subject of the next chapter.

Quality of Couple Relationship

Some of the women described relationships which were very good for several years. They described being 'best pals' (Catherine) with their husbands and how, for most of their married lives, they had never considered that they might separate. They described how supportive their husbands were when they went back to study (Irene) and when they were sick (Nora). These are good examples of love and care being done in a manner which built connectedness and made the women feel loved.

NORA: We got on well. We always spoke about everything, you know. I couldn't say anything. Billy was a very easy person to get on with. In 2006, I got breast cancer and he was very good to me. The girls said he cried when I was in having surgery. And he didn't know what to do and what if anything happened me and all of this.

Jane described how shocked their family and friends were when she and her husband separated because they were seen as such a united couple.

JANE: When our marriage broke up we were the shock of the century, we were THE shock. We were the Waltons[1] one second, if you know, we did everything together, the lads were big into sport, we travelled everywhere with them. We did everything as a family, you know.

Jane, Nora, Irene and Catherine felt they had good relationships with their husbands. They felt connected to them over many years of marriage and did not think that they would separate. On balance, they felt that their marriages were 'good enough'. The separations in these cases came about as a result of infidelity by their husbands and came as a shock to the women.

Sexual Relations

McDonnell (1999) identified sexual problems within a marriage as barometer issues which signified deeper problems in marriages. The women in the study seemed to agree with this interpretation of sexual problems as a symptom rather than as a cause of relationship difficulties. Deirdre states that the absence of sex was one of a range of distancing behaviours, all of which affected each other. Initially, practical reasons were given for the absence of sex, for example, that the man was working nights (Anne) or because the man snored so much (Deirdre) or because the man had become obese and had sleep apnoea (Irene).

---

1   The 'Waltons' is an American television series which depicts a rural family in which relationships are invariably wholesome and loving.

L: When you started to sleep in separate bedrooms, was that your choice or his choice or did you think, now we are really in trouble?

ANNE: No, that was going on a long time because Noel had very erratic habits. He would never kind of go to bed at eleven and get up at eight. He didn't have that type of a lifestyle. He worked shift hours and he would stay up late at night. I'd be up in the morning and had to be going with the children. So that was how that started.

L: Very different sleeping patterns. There was no real intimacy, closeness?

ANNE: No. There wasn't for a long time.

L: Sometimes when resentment builds up one of the things that happens is that there is no sex. Did Brendan ever come back into the bedroom after he had left when your second baby was born?

DEIRDRE: Yes he did but I was the one who left the bedroom. I left the bedroom very gradually and initially it was because of snoring.

L: Was it [you moving to the spare room] something you could talk about to your husband?

DEIRDRE: Not really. It was to do with his snoring. I tried to see would he do something about that. It came up again during the counselling. It's very hard to separate what was causing what. It's a whole combination.

L: Were you still having sex at that stage? Were you still sharing a bed?

IRENE: Yes, we were. I think I had given him the cold shoulder many times because I'll tell you what happened. George got very obese, put on an awful lot of weight. I was worried about his blood pressure because it was sky high. He had sleep apnoea. He had insomnia and I was sleeping beside this guy whom I could hear stopping breathing. He was terrible at snoring because he was so fat. So really I wasn't a happy camper with this person. This was not the person I had lived a lot of my life with.

A pattern of not having sex started gradually and for practical reasons. It then became the norm in the couples' marriages, without any discussion taking place about what was happening or how each partner felt about the absence of sex. Irene also linked the absence of sex with the fact that her husband had changed so much. This sense of partners becoming strangers to each other is a common theme in literature on relationships (Bateson, 2000).

Deirdre and Helen described the shame they would have felt if anyone knew they were not having sex and that they continued to share a bed in order to keep up appearances in front of the children or if their family members were visiting.

DEIRDRE: There was nearly a stigma attached. I thought if anyone knew that we didn't stay in the same room, that it was scandalous. If my mother ever came down to stay, I was in that bedroom with him regardless of what went on every other night.

L: Sometimes when communication goes, sex goes. Was that an issue? Was it gone?
HELEN: It was gone.
L: Did Jim initiate that or did you initiate it? Did you have separate bedrooms?
HELEN: Not until the end, or near enough to the end. I was thinking of everybody else. I didn't want the children to see. I put up with him.

The common scenario described was that sexual relations had ceased as a consequence of the deterioration in communication and disengaging that had been taking place over several years. Emotional distancing had been taking place so, to the women, it made sense that physical distancing was also taking place. They were not feeling loved so they were not showing love in a physical manner.

However, some of the women were still having sex with their husband right up to the time of their separations.

L: Did you go to separate bedrooms?
KAY: Oh no, and that would never have happened, never. And sex wouldn't have been wonderful all the time, but, no that would never have happened.
L: No, you would never have done that, or suggested or felt ...
KAY: No never, never. No, Brian was my husband. And you know for twenty years it had been a very, very satisfying relationship.

Sarah, on the other hand, felt that sexual problems had been a primary cause in the breakdown of her marriage.

SARAH: I again, was trying to keep the sex life going, and he just one day said, 'for God's sake Sarah, this has to stop,' he said, 'we're too old,' he said 'I'm fifty,' and I said, 'Ken I'm only forty-seven, I don't feel I'm too old,' and he said 'well I just feel that we're too old,' and I remember I just turned and I said, 'ok, that is that, that's the nail in the coffin, I am never going to put myself out there again.'

The rejection Sarah felt and her sense of not feeling loved are recurring themes in many of the quotations. As with almost every theme in this discussion, there are differences in the sexual relationships described by the women. Some were still having sex almost right up to the time they separated. Others were still sleeping in the same beds but not having sex. Others had long since moved to separate bedrooms. Three of the women alluded to the possibility that their husbands might have been gay. Another woman's husband disclosed, twenty years into their marriage, that he had been abused as a child. The common denominator in all cases was that the couples were unable or unwilling to discuss these matters. A gulf in understanding and an inability to connect truly with each other emerged as a result of failing to deal with a very difficult issue.

Approaches to Resolving Conflict

How couples resolve conflict has been found to be a key factor in the success or failure of many marriages (McKeown *et al.*, 2004). Again the issue of how girls and boys are socialised to deal with conflict is relevant. Some of the women felt that they had been brought up to be quiet and submissive. Messages internalised from childhood about the importance of self-denial for women and about 'not being worthy' (Inglis, 2008) may have had a bearing. The women felt that if there was a confrontation on matters that were bothering them, they were accused of 'rocking the boat'. Many of them felt their husbands did not have the ability to discuss emotionally difficult topics. Therefore, the women felt they were being pressurised into being silent and into not causing rows. Many of the women blamed themselves for not being more assertive. They felt unable to bring about change. Fighting did not work. Silence did not work. They were unable to communicate or to find a method that was effective for resolving their problems.

Anne, Frances and Geraldine were not passive types. They described how they used to 'lose their cool' or 'stand their ground'.

> ANNE: If I lost my cool and gave out in a row, I was losing it (according to him). I wasn't allowed to bang a door. 'Calm down there. You're the one that's losing their cool here. You're out of order'.

> FRANCES: I used to get really angry. I used to blow at him. I would be the type of person that I would get quite excitable, about good things and bad things in equal measure. I would react and so I used to get really annoyed.

GERALDINE: There were rows, big rows as well and that's what upset the kids because I always stood my ground. But Tom knew that if he riled me that I would react that way so it was this vicious circle, big fights, loud shouting rows coming towards the end. But at the time I tried to keep the rows, as much as I could, away from the children but he started dragging them into the same room as the kids, that way I couldn't get to him. I wouldn't be able to say what I wanted to say so he knew that was how to get me. So I had to say what I had to say. I couldn't change my behaviour, it didn't suit. That way the kids were witnessing the fights. It was awful, it was awful. That went on for years.

Deirdre, Helen, Eileen and Sarah described how silence and withdrawal were the methods of conflict resolution used in their houses. There is a common theme in the accounts that follow of the women being reluctant to say what was upsetting them for fear it would lead to a row which would invariably be followed by a protracted period of silence.

DEIRDRE: Here at home, when I was annoyed with him (it's probably one of the worst ways to deal with it) but silence was my answer for it. Silence would build up for long periods of time. If there was a row or a disagreement over something, Brendan would carry a silence on for days, whereas I would be inclined to go silent too, but it would go out of my system more quickly. I would find myself often pussy-footing around him saying 'I'd better be careful what I say around him, I'd better not ask him to cut the grass, because he won't do it and that will cause a row and then there'll be a long silence'.

L: Did you go silent if you were bothered by something?
HELEN: Jim would as well and he would just back away. In fairness, as well, I now realise that I wouldn't bring up stuff as well because I'd know what the conflict was like. I now know that that was wrong and it should have been all brought to the fore. That was the big thing, that problem stemmed from communication.

In other relationships, if something contentious arose, it did not lead to a row because both spouses withdrew into silence rather than into conflict or fighting.

L: Very often, if people disagree, they compromise.

EILEEN: I think women compromise. I compromised all the way along. I was this quiet person who made sure the boat didn't rock. If I disagreed, David just disappeared so there was no communication. I wasn't heard. If I disagreed, he disappeared and came back and said nothing. I just shut down. If I disagreed or said anything emotional, he withdrew. He didn't want to know about it.

SARAH: I learned that if I pushed that Ken would get annoyed, and he would withdraw his love or he would become remote, and that was hard to deal with. Or he might say something snippy, you know, so you learn not to rock the boat. And because that was a bit my personality anyway, don't rock the boat, it was familiar territory. So you just hide it and you get on with it, and you cry a little bit at night, the little tears come out, but you get on with it because you have the girls and you can't ...

The methods of conflict resolution referred to are similar to those described in literature on typical strategies people utilise when trying to resolve conflict in relationships (McKeown *et al.*, 2003), except that there is no mention of any physical violence by any of the women in this study. Investing the required time and effort into resolving conflict is a key aspect of showing love (Lynch, 2007). It requires people to be honest and assertive, at the same time as being empathic. It requires people to take a problem-solving approach to what is a joint problem. Using violence and aggression are the least effective and most damaging methods of attempting to resolve conflict (McKeown, *et al.*, 2003). Silence and withdrawal avoid the worst excesses of the aggressive approach but, as these women have described, the silent approach may eventually lead to a gradual distancing or fragmenting of the relationship. Silence and withdrawal can be interpreted as rejection and as not caring enough or not having the skills to do the work required to talk through the issues that lead to the conflict in the first place. By their own admission, a number of the women blamed themselves partially for not being courageous enough to follow through on confronting issues in a more assertive manner.

Awareness of Gradual Deterioration of Relationships

Some marriages were described as having been in difficulties for years. The themes that emerged from these descriptions referred to the women not feeling emotionally close to their husbands, not feeling loved or cared for, but not feeling that they could either 'mend or end' their marriages (McKeown *et al.*, 2004) and so continuing to live in very unhappy situations for several years. Deirdre and Sarah identified emotional distancing and lack of closeness and affection as the problems. Mary outlined how the breakdown of communication lead to a breakdown in trust which then resulted in most communication between spouses being negative or aggressive.

> DEIRDRE: I mean it was just a gradual, bit by bit, deterioration. He started going out a lot on his own. When I attempted to find out where was he going, why was he going out, I got answers like 'you don't seem to really care about me so you don't need to know these things and its nothing to do with you really'.

> SARAH: I ended up crying a lot and not knowing why I was crying, and really deep inside me I knew the kernel was the relationship was not great and I was afraid to voice that, put words on that because I would have to do something about it or face it, and I knew I couldn't. Because it wasn't bad enough, there was no reason, he wasn't being unfaithful, I wasn't being unfaithful. There was no physical abuse or that. But there was slowly starting this emotional distancing. So gradually over the next few years, I started disengaging. He disengaged first emotionally. I started protecting myself, putting up the wall.

> MARY: I think we stopped probably really talking to each other in a way about what we felt. I think it's about acknowledging each other's feelings and being able to say what you're feeling. It got to the point where we kind of stopped talking to each other. I think that was the biggest factor. I think that probably was the biggest thing. The communication just breaks down somehow and then the trust goes as well because then the communication is often only angry or negative communication, name calling and that kind of stuff.

Deirdre, Sarah and Mary are describing a gradual disconnecting in their relationships with their husbands. In hindsight, they could see that there had been problems for several years, but the prospect of separation was so frightening and so at odds with the ideology about marriage that they had grown up with, that they struggled to acknowledge the problem either to themselves or to others. Conceiving of separation as a solution to their marital problems took time to process.

The emphasis on relational issues is a common theme in the literature on the causes that women, in particular, are found to identify as the reasons for their divorces (Amato and Previti, 2003). Women were more likely than men to refer to emotional or relational issues. Not feeling emotionally close to their partners and not feeling that emotions were reciprocated emerged as common themes in several of the studies reviewed (McDonnell, 1999; Wolcott and Hughes, 1999; O'Connor, 2001; Amato and Previti, 2003; McKeown *et al.*, 2004).

Attendance at Marriage Counselling

Given the difficulties in the marriages described up to this point, attendance at marriage counselling services was an option that couples would be expected to utilise. Just six (Anne, Catherine, Deirdre, Geraldine, Kay and Mary) of the fourteen couples attended marriage counselling at a stage prior to consideration of separation.

Anne and Kay described how they felt blamed and 'under attack' during the counselling sessions.

> ANNE: It was a private counsellor. It was about the marriage but Noel did say he had a problem with drinking and when the counsellor heard that she said 'well look now that needs to be dealt with, that's a separate issue' ... Then she was saying 'oh focus on the communication' and this sort of thing. Now I did make an effort. She was saying we should make the time and we should make a little list. I was blue in the face trying to make this communication work. But a lot of the time things were being thrown back on me. I was getting the blame for everything ...

> KAY: So we went for counselling, but counselling just shocked me because I felt Brian was just there to criticise me all the time ... But at some stage in the end I said, 'no, this is not working for me,' because I just felt under attack all the time there.

Deirdre and Geraldine felt that counselling worked for a while but that the same problems re-emerged quickly once the counselling sessions ended.

> DEIRDRE: We went to counselling more than once. It was my suggestion. I made the phone call. We went privately in another town because we wanted to get away from here and we went up there for a while. It gave us both the opportunity to say what we wanted to say and we took it all on board and I suppose we came home and things started getting back to the way they were before.
>
> L: You said you went to counselling more than once.
>
> DEIRDRE: I went to individual counselling for myself and that lady suggested that we try going as a couple for a while. Again we did and it was the same thing, each of us sharing our own feelings and yet nothing changed ...

> GERALDINE: We saw this woman for a while, it must have been about three or four months, it helped a bit. We spoke a bit more but when it came to doing exercises, he wouldn't do them. He wasn't that engaged in the process at all.

Mary and Pat began counselling when they lived abroad. Like Anne and Geraldine, Mary states that her husband would not follow through on completing the exercises set as 'homework' to be completed between sessions. Geraldine interpreted this as meaning that her husband was not really engaged in the process of trying to save their marriage.

> MARY: In the couples' counselling we would always reach an impasse where we couldn't go beyond, we just couldn't work through some of the issues. The counsellor suggested doing different sessions, different group things but in the end, to be fair neither of us are great at group things and he really didn't want to do it and the exercises she would give us to do we would never get them done and it just got to the point where we weren't making any progress so we stopped going to counselling.

Catherine's experience of counselling was more positive and long term.

> L: Women typically seek to mend or end relationships. Did you suggest going to counselling?
>
> CATHERINE: Yes, we went to different sessions over the years and we would come back together quite quickly (the last time this happened was ten years ago), after about eight or nine months ... At that time we went to family counselling ... We didn't go for many sessions and he came home and the eight years had been very good.

Research into the outcomes of counselling by O' Connor (2001) found that 15% of service users felt their problems were resolved, 32% felt their problems were still present but that they were coping better and 25% felt their problems were unresolved. The experience of the couples in this study locates them within the group for whom counselling was successful in the short-term. What most of the women said was that counselling worked for a while but that relationships reverted back over time to how they had been before.

It is typically women who initiate marriage counselling (McKeown *et al.*, 2002; 2004 and O' Connor, 2001). Several of the women who did not attend as a couple stated that their husbands had refused to attend and that they had attended on their own. Again, there is a gendered theme coming through about some of the men's inability or resistance to engaging in discussion about emotionally difficult topics.

Significant Events: Turning Points

The events that the women pinpointed as being significant in their eventual separations were events that occurred during family holidays or at times of illness or death in the family. The common theme in all the stories that were told about these events was how unloved the women felt as a result of how their husbands behaved at those times.

Holidays

Lack of closeness in marital relationships was felt especially on holidays and during family celebrations. It would appear that the change from busy daily schedules showed up relationships' difficulties in a clearer light. On holidays, the expectation is that couples have a good time together, enjoy each other's company, have sex, enjoy seeing new things and meeting new people, away from the stresses and strains of work. If the opposite happens, then it is more obvious that a relationship is in trouble than may be apparent in the course of a normal weekly routine, as Geraldine described:

GERALDINE: Now the first time I really, finally saw that there was a problem was in '97. I remember the year because we were away on holiday. We took the ferry to Wales. On the way down to get the boat a bus sliced a chunk out of our car and didn't stop, just kept going. It was half seven in the morning and we were trying to get the boat. That was the start of the beginning of the end. There were rows for the whole time and I tried not to get annoyed but then on the boat on the way home, the second fella fell out of one of the bunks and slit his head open and we had to get that treated on the boat. It was just things like that. It was that kind of a holiday, a lot of tension, little small accidents happening and just one massive row.

L: Had you been taking family holidays together?

HELEN: Yes, the last one we took was that June and it was the biggest nightmare. It was hell on earth. We were going to France. We decided, as part of our holiday, we'd take in Paris for four or five days and I asked my parents to come with us. Communication was still kind of going on between us at this stage but he was a 'mentler'. I was trying to hide everything from everybody. Jim really was so rude to my parents. And then my parents went home and we went up into Brittany and we were in a very remote place and I hadn't got insured in the car, he was just desperate. I thought I would never get home. He hardly spoke to us. I was trying to keep the whole thing going with just two of the girls.

Helen was clearly still trying to present the image of being a happy family to her parents and to her children. Keeping up appearances was important. The obvious problem whereby her husband barely spoke to her and the children and was rude to her parents was not confronted.

Coping with Illness and Death

A number of the women described coping with illness, either their own, their husbands', their children's or their parents' as being particularly stressful.

BREDA: Well I suppose the biggest issue was that shortly after we got married my husband was diagnosed with diabetes, the type where he was injecting insulin every day. And he would be your typical man who would not talk about it ... He wouldn't carry anything to say that he had diabetes, which was sort of alright in the beginning because he was young and fit. But, diabetes, as it progresses, starts to affect all the organs ... When you live with someone who has a life-threatening illness, it causes stress.

Lack of emotional closeness and support was felt more acutely at times when the women, their children or their parents were ill as Deirdre describes:

> DEIRDRE: I suffered the greatest pain that I never, ever want to go back there again. I just couldn't get up off the floor. I went into the bathroom and I said to him 'oh I hurt my back'. Every bit of blood drained out of me. I went into the bathroom and I got sick with the pain. Brendan turned over in the bed and he said 'oh you better get back into bed'. Now that was one of the coldest, cruellest things I can ever remember. At that stage, things weren't very bad but that stuck with me. He didn't even sit up in the bed to see was I sitting or standing or lying. I thought I was going to faint and I never fainted in my life and he said 'well, you'd better get back into bed'.

Lack of emotional closeness and support was also felt more acutely at times of bereavements. If love was not felt at times of loss, its absence was even more apparent than that experienced in the normal course of daily living. Carter and McGoldrick (2005) identify that coming to terms with the deaths of parents or, less commonly, with the death of siblings is one of the key tasks for people during midlife.

> EILEEN: The emotional support was never there. One of the things that keeps coming into my mind was the time my brother died and when I walked in the door, all I wanted was a hug and David just walked away. My brother had just died but no.

> MARY: My brother died all of a sudden, he had a brain haemorrhage, 56 years old and died in a week. So somehow I agreed to let Pat come back and I think at the time it was because I just couldn't cope with my brother dying. I literally couldn't hold it together so I just said 'fine'.

Several of the women mentioned the deaths of their parents or their parents-in-law as particularly stressful times in their lives which may have had an effect on the subsequent deterioration of their relationships. For Anne and Deirdre, these deaths happened around the same time as their first children were born which added additional stress at that time.

ANNE: Both of my parents died in 1989. They both passed away the one year. I was pretty cut up, especially over my mother. My father had had a lot of illness and a stroke and a heart attack so that wasn't as much of a shock. My mother died six months after so that was a cruel shock. But then my son was born. With my parents after passing away and a new child, I was so focussed on them that I probably wasn't focussing too much on Noel I wouldn't say at the time. He had then become rather unwell.

DEIRDRE: My father became ill and died. Brendan's father died on a Friday and my father died the next day, he died within twenty four hours. And there were illnesses leading up to it so that strain was there as well. Not long after our son was born, his mother became very ill and, I felt, it was a combination of all of those things, that, little by little by little, they were chipping away at the relationship. There just wasn't time. We didn't have the skills to know that we still needed to work at our own relationship, take care of ourselves ... that just wasn't there.

A number of the women linked the timing of their separations to the deaths of either their parents or their husbands' parents. Sarah was shocked by both of her parents dying within three weeks of each other. At around the same time she also reached a 'milestone' birthday of fifty years of age which she described as finding very difficult. Both events caused her to re-consider how she wanted to live the rest of her life.

SARAH: They died three weeks apart actually, which was horrendous ... In that April I turned 50, it was the time that my mother was very ill and we thought that she was going to die and I really, really noticed the lack of support from him and, not there for me really at all.

Helen felt that her husband stayed with her and the children until such time as his mother died because he knew his mother would be very upset if he separated from his wife.

HELEN: His mother died in 2005. It was 2006 when we separated. Somebody said something about what would his mother have thought and the way he was treating the children. He said 'I wouldn't have done it while she was still alive'. It was more or less he waited 'til she died.

It seems to be part of the story of separation that people can identify, in retrospect, key 'turning points' along the way. The women were not asked specifically about holidays, illnesses or bereavements but they recounted stories about these events to illustrate particular incidents in their marriages which signalled that they were in serious difficulty.

Discussion: Problems with Love and Care in Marriage

It appears that some of the women lived for years, decades even, in marriages where there was very little emotional closeness. There was 'passive neglect' of relationships (Aronson *et al.*, 2003) but reluctance to proactively seek to either mend or end the marriages (McKeown *et al.*, 2004). A minimum amount of love and care was being done which was sufficient to maintain the outward appearance or 'shell' of a marriage but the shell had long since become empty. The shell offered some protection. It was familiar. It had the appearance of being like everybody else's shell. Living outside it was not the norm and was almost unthinkable for this age group of women. They were loyal to the ideal of life-long marriage and were very reluctant to give voice to how unhappy they were in their marriages. Marriage counselling worked in the short term for some, but in most cases the men refused to go to counselling, until it was too late. Some couples did not engage in the dyadic phase of the break-up (Duck, 1998).

Awareness that love and care were not present was particularly apparent during holidays or at times of illness or bereavement. Behaviours on these occasions were seen as being more actively destructive (Rusbult *et al.*, 1996) than the passive neglect which was witnessed on a daily basis. It took events like these to show that marriages were in serious trouble and that love and care were not being shown by one or both of the marriage partners. Connectedness through acts of loving and caring was a key expectation of marriage for the women in this study. Where love and care failed to be shown, problems ensued and fragmentation or dissolution of relationships began to occur. Couples entered the exit quadrant of Rusbult's (1996) typology.

CHAPTER 6

Events and Feelings at the Time of Separation

This chapter presents and analyses data on the events and processes that occurred around the time of separation. (The data are summarised in Appendix 2.) Lengthy excerpts from all fourteen interviews are included because it was important for the women to outline in detail their reasons for initiating separation or the circumstances surrounding how they learned about their husbands' infidelity. The chapter continues the focus on the second research question concerning the events and processes that lead to separation and also discusses the third question about the losses experienced while transitioning through separation.

Transition and Loss

Carter and McGoldrick (2005) conceptualise divorce as an 'unscheduled' transition in a family life-cycle. Ahrons (2005) describes transitions as 'turning points, uncomfortable periods that mark the beginning of something new while signifying the ending of something familiar' (p. 384). The focus in this chapter is on the event of separating and on the losses associated with the ending of 'something familiar'.

Separation and divorce involve several losses (Ahrons, 2005). There is the loss of a life style, the loss of identity as part of a couple, the loss of a partner, the loss of what is considered to be an intact family, the loss of friendships associated with being married and the loss of a future together. These losses are similar to those experienced by a bereaved spouse. The difference between bereavement and separation is that separation often also involves feelings of rejection and betrayal and results from 'a deliberate dissolution' of the couple relationship (Ahrons, 2005: 385). There are no communal rituals to support the people who are separating. There are few adequate role models to show the way. There is a void and an ambiguity about the manner in which to behave and to make this transition (Carter and McGoldrick, 2005).

Woman as Initiator of the Ending of a Marriage

Literature on women's experience of separation often distinguishes between women who initiate separation, women who are non-initiators and those who separate by mutual agreement (Sakraida, 2005). In her study in Indiana, Sakraida found that instances where separation appeared to be by agreement, had actually been initiated by one person and the other person had reluctantly agreed. She questioned whether or not the decision to separate ever truly occurs by agreement. Only one (Mary) of the fourteen women in this study came close to separating by agreement. Separation by mutual agreement is not, therefore, a key area for discussion in this text.

A deliberate decision was made at the start of this study to include women who were initiators of separation as well as women who were non-initiators. The intention was to try to capture the experience of separation from a woman's perspective, as a gendered experience, regardless of the specific circumstances that led to the separation. Deciding whether a woman is an initiator or a non-initiator of separation is not as simple as it may first appear. Court records show that women initiate court proceedings for separation more often than men (Coulter, 2008). This does not necessarily mean that more women than men want to separate. Women may need to sort out arrangements for children and money at an early stage which is the reason they are the ones who generally initiate legal proceedings (Coulter, 2008). A number of the women asked their husbands to leave after they learned that the men were having affairs, but prior to that discovery the women had not been planning to separate. So even though the women were the ones who asked the men to leave, they did not consider themselves to be the initiators of their separations.

The approach taken in this study was to invite the women to identify themselves as either initiators or non-initiators. Of the fourteen women interviewed, six (Anne, Breda, Deirdre, Eileen, Frances and Sarah) identified themselves as having initiated their separations. The process by which they arrived at the decision to separate was often slow and protracted.

> DEIRDRE: I still remember that lady (counsellor) saying to me 'if you don't do something about this, you will become very ill'. She frightened the life out of me about the effect it could have on my health. I did what I did to look after myself and to get myself out of a situation that was going to basically destroy me if I didn't go ... I hung on with the children in mind for a long time ... The first time that I thought that this had to be done or when I came to the conclusion that this was not going to fix itself, was probably maybe three/four years before I actually did it. There was either one of them doing their Leaving Cert. or one of them was moving into college or there seemed to be always some reason why this was not a good year. Whether that was me putting it off or out of genuine concern for them, I don't know.

> EILEEN: Three years before I left I spoke to him and said how I felt and it was back to normal the next day. Nothing was taken on board of what I said ... I just got so, so low. I just thought 'I don't want to live like this for the rest of my life'. I just thought 'I can't take this anymore. I can't take being told what I can and can't do' ... I have seen family members suffer and dying young through illness. I said 'I don't want to die because of my marriage'. I started to listen to myself. I allowed myself to be angry. I realised how invisible I was and that really I didn't matter, once I was there every evening to put food on the table and to just sit with him, that's all he wanted ... But nobody knew. Nobody ever knew how I felt. I did actually think about leaving five years before but I still had a child at school.

> SARAH: I actually used to pray 'if only he would meet someone'. That would take the decision out of my hands. So about four years before that I went to ring a solicitor. I talked it over with a friend of mine and I decided 'no I can't. I have six years to go until the youngest is eighteen. I can do six years, I will do those. I will not have it on my conscience that I upset her life'.

The common theme in these quotations is how unhappy the women were in their marriages but that they were prepared to wait until a time when the effect on their children might be less severe. Sarah uses the phrase 'doing six years' as if she were serving a prison sentence.

Frances, on the other hand, indicated that she had initiated separation when she and her husband reached an impasse about how and where they wanted to live for the rest of their lives. He wanted to sell their house, clear their debts and move to a different part of the country. The move would have taken them away from their children, her job and friends and she was not prepared to move. She felt it was an unreasonable request and that it spelled the end of their marriage. She was the first one to mention the word 'separate'.

> FRANCES: The bills were mounting up on the hall table until there were about sixty letters and he wouldn't open them. He just never bothered. Then he came up with this brilliant brain-wave that we'd sell up.
> L: Sell your family home?
> FRANCES: Sell our home so that we'd have no debts. So I said 'no, I couldn't do that' and he just said 'well, that's what I need to do'. I said 'well then the only solution is to separate'. I was business-like about it.

At the time, Frances stated she was 'business-like' about the decision that she and her husband needed to go their separate ways, but this does not mean that she found the process easy or that it did not entail regret and a sense of loss. She outlined how many unanswered questions she was left with:

> FRANCES: I often ask myself 'if I loved him enough, would I have gone? And if he loved me enough, would he have stayed? Would he have put the gun to my head?

Breda, likewise, reached an impasse with her husband and was the first one to use the word 'separation'.

> L: Was it you who mentioned the possibility of separating first?
> BREDA: I initiated the whole lot.
> L: With anger?
> BREDA: With huge anger. But even now I would say it was not what I wanted ... But I made the decision at the time because I felt it was in my best interests and, particularly, in my daughter's best interests. I agonised over it. Sure, I tormented myself ...
> L: Once you made a decision, was that it?
> BREDA: I would have gone back on it if he had given me the slightest indication ...

It is clear that the women who initiated separation did not arrive at the decision lightly. The gradual deterioration of relationships and the emotional distancing from partners led to the women's decisions to separate from their husbands. These decisions were motivated for most of the women by fears that their physical or mental health would break down if they stayed. The women's decisions to separate related to a basic need to survive rather than being motivated by a desire for 'self-actualisation' or 'individualisation'.

Sudden Endings: Wife as Initiator

Some of the separations happened very abruptly. After years of unhappiness, matters came to a head and ended in a matter of days. Anne described a row about a radiator and who was going to drive her son to the bus as 'the straw that broke the camel's back'.

> ANNE: And then the straw that broke the camel's back, believe it or not, was a very small thing ... He said I was turning off the heating in his bedroom ... I'd already asked him to drive my son and he didn't want to do that because he was drinking. That was a dreadful day in our house ... And my daughter was there listening to all this row about the radiator, row about the lifts. It was awful for her. She said 'can we not go somewhere for a break?' I said 'I think we will go somewhere for a break'.

Breda described her husband's refusal to help her daughter prepare for the Special Olympics as the 'tipping point'.

> BREDA: It was the time of the Special Olympics. It was a big event. My daughter might never get married, she might never have children ... He would not get involved. He would not even take her training. In hindsight, of course, he was actually quite ill at the time ... I have no way of knowing the reason why he was reluctant to get involved.
> L: His reluctance to get involved was one of the factors that led to your decision to separate?
> BREDA: Yes, it was the deciding factor. What I would call the 'tipping point', what tipped me over. I was incredibly stressed at the time, too much on my plate. I tried to talk to him about it ...

Each woman remembered clearly the details of the encounters on the day the decision to separate was first discussed with their husbands.

> DEIRDRE: I can still see the day that I said it to him. He was lighting the fire in there and I came in from school. He must have been off work for the day and I just blurted it out. I said 'we can't go on like this. I want to separate'.

> EILEEN: When I was asked if I wanted to go on holiday and I thought 'I can't do this anymore, I can't do this anymore'. So after a few minutes I said 'no, I don't want to go'. A few days later, we were to go to a wedding and I said 'I don't want to go to the wedding, in actual fact, I want a break'. He said he didn't expect that reply and, as it happened, we had to go to a funeral several days later and I was back in the normal role ... Then when I spoke after we came back from that he said he thought everything was normal.
> L: So he was in a place where he was saying 'let's go on a holiday together' and you were in a place where you were saying 'I'm out of here. I can't do this anymore'.
> EILEEN: Yes, total mismatch of where we were at. I acted the part. I have to say, I was acting a part for so long and he just expected me to continue.

> SARAH: So the way it happened was he was buying a new dining room table which was all going to cost two or three thousand, a big, old mahogany thing, and I said, 'Ken I don't want you to buy that', and I kind of knew I was only going to get one chance to say this, and he said 'why?' and I kind of rehearsed it, 'because there is no point in buying a new dining room table if there is only one of you to use it', and he said 'what do you mean', and I said, 'I want a separation'.

It is not hard to imagine the men's shock in these situations if this was the first time separation was discussed. One man was unsuspectingly lighting the fire, another man was planning a holiday and a day out at a wedding and the third man was thinking about investing in a new dining room table. Where the wife was the person who initiated the separation, it seemed to come as a total shock to the husbands. They had not seen it coming. They had not dreamed that their wives would ever go so far as to leave. There seems to have been a disconnection between the person who was considering leaving and the person who was about to be left. It seems to be an accumulation of the communication difficulties and distancing that were features of so many of the marriages. These couples had been failing to communicate for years. They had failed to talk, to listen or to make themselves heard, so perhaps it is not surprising that they had failed to communicate that they were thinking of leaving.

> BREDA: I don't think he believed it until a solicitor's letter came in the door.

> SARAH: Either he wasn't listening or didn't have the capacity to process it emotionally. Well it was news to him. He started to cry, and I was very perplexed by that. He'd no idea, and I said 'but how could you not have any idea?' 'Oh, I just thought that was just you and the change of life' and he went into a big depression and didn't know what to do.

What is emerging is a huge gulf in understanding between spouses on fundamental issues such as what each person wanted from the relationship and how distressed and hurt they were when, as they saw it, their expectations of a loving and caring relationship were not being met. It was as though one person had already left the marriage for years before they discussed their decision with the other person and that they then just presumed that the other person 'knew'. The reason the husbands did not 'know' was because they had not understood how unhappy their wives were. It had not occurred to them that their wives might leave.

Endings Due to Infidelity

Infidelity is a common cause of separation (Wolcott and Hughes, 1999; Amato, 2000; Lowenstein, 2007). According to Subotnik and Harris (2005), there are different types of affairs and different types of infidelity. There are 'serial affairs, flings, romantic love affairs, and long-term affairs' (p. iii). There are emotional affairs which do not involve touching but which constitute emotional infidelity. There are sexual affairs which do not involve emotions and there are affairs which involve both sex and emotional investment. It is the meaning the other spouse attaches to the infidelity which determines the decision made about the marriage. Subotnik and Harris (2005) suggest that a person's life stage also has an impact on the decision they make about the marriage. 'We have seen older women who have looked the other way when extra-marital involvement occurred

rather than risk age-bias in the job market or worry about living alone'
(p. 118). Looking the other way was not the option chosen by most of the
women in this study, as their stories will illustrate.

Six (Catherine, Geraldine, Helen, Irene, Jane and Nora) of the fourteen
women identified their husbands' sexual or emotional infidelity as being
the precipitating reason for their separations. In Catherine's case, the issue
was emotional infidelity. Her husband worked mostly with women and
had a pattern of developing very close friendships with particular women
but concealing details of contacts from his wife. A similar series of events
lead to a period apart eight years previously.

> CATHERINE: We were away for a month. I discovered stuff that he was buying and
> I just curled up in a ball ... My sister said 'let it go. It'll spin itself out.' I remember
> the June weekend, we were away down the country and she said 'I take it all back.
> I don't know how you can let that go'. He went off down the lane from the cottage
> we were staying in to talk on the phone ... I asked him time and time again and he
> said 'no'. I felt out of my mind. I felt humiliated. I told him to leave.

It is not unusual for couples to separate for periods of time and to come
back together again before, in some cases, separating permanently. For these
couples, a series of prior separations is part of the story of their experiences
of separation. Like Catherine, Nora had been through previous separations
from her husband. On the first occasion she was totally shocked when he
told her he was leaving for a woman he had met on a training course.

> NORA: All of a sudden, she was his soul-mate. She had already been in a previous life
> of his and they were meant to be together ... He wasn't having an affair. This woman
> was a soul-mate but he wasn't having an affair with her at the time.

The relationship ended after a few months and Nora took her husband
back, only for the same thing to happen again some years later with a different woman.

In all six cases of infidelity, the women described how in retrospect
they could track the signs that their relationships had been deteriorating.
The build-up to the women finding out or to the men disclosing their affairs
was characterised by the men spending very little time at home. Because of

the lies, deceit and denials involved in these cases, there were many unanswered questions and many pieces of information missing. This resulted in the women struggling to make sense of what had been happening and how long the affairs had been going on.

In Geraldine's case, her husband had had a previous affair but had said it was over. Out of the blue she got a phone call to say he was in hospital.

> GERALDINE: He said he had been up all night trying to figure out the best way to top himself. During the course of that six week programme he took me aside and said 'I want to separate' ... It materialised that he was in a relationship. He had been in this relationship for a number of years. This girl, actually, she was our former au pair ... The night before he left to move in with her he said 'ah no, we're friends. We email each other occasionally'. And then he left. He had already put a deposit on an apartment ... He still had the keys because I was at college. He came back to make the dinner. He was serving out the spaghetti, the kids were coming out from the sitting room, 'oh by the way now, it's over and she's moved in'. That was it. That was how I heard. That's my story.

Jane is still unsure if her husband was having a sexual affair. His extremely negative reaction when she asked him about it was what made her suspicious.

> JANE: This girl joined the club. She was playing with him on a Monday night. Tuesday and Thursday nights they coached together, and she began coaching with him on Saturday mornings, and taking the kids off to trips ... So this day his phone beeped, and I read a message. 'I can meet you for a few minutes' – and it was her. So I discovered he had two numbers for her in his phone, so my stomach just hit the ground ... and I said 'if you are having an affair would you tell me.' Well a monster, a monster appeared here. I never saw anything like it, his whole face went disfigured, and 'no, no, no'. I said 'just wondering' and I said nothing. So the next day I asked him, would he get a phone bill ... He never produced the phone bill ... he told me he was ringing men and women on sex lines. Now, I don't know if that was just an excuse ... There's a lot of unanswered things ... To this day he denies it saying 'there's nothing, you know, but she was my best friend' ... I'd say there was more to it, though, because, this girl had done something like this before.

Helen, similar to Jane, became suspicious that her husband was having an affair and started looking for evidence.

HELEN: He just started withdrawing, withdrawing, withdrawing. He wouldn't come home ... I now know he was having the affair at that stage. And he still, to this day, has not admitted that to anybody. I had suspected and I started going through his stuff and I found receipts and visa bills for accommodation. He was supposed to have been abroad working and I found receipts for another part of Ireland where he was and all this type of stuff. I did say it to him and he made a laugh out of me and made a mockery out of me.

The first indication Irene had that her husband was having an affair was when he told her that he was leaving her. He initially denied that he was having an affair but he flew to Spain the next day with another woman.

IRENE: George said to me that we needed to talk and that he was going to leave now that my youngest daughter had reached eighteen and that he wanted a new life before he died, that he had lived my life and that was it, he was leaving. I remember we were walking down the canal. We went out for walks all the time. I said 'so who is involved? What are you going to do?' He said 'there's nobody involved.' But I knew from the beginning that there was no return because I found tickets on his desk that were booked to Spain the day after he told me. So it was well planned. I found the tickets, paid by somebody else's credit card. I thought 'everybody knows, oh my god, everybody knows'. It was a terrible feeling that I didn't twig this. Betrayal like this I cannot stomach. He has hurt me so much. He has hurt the kids which is ten times the hurt for me, feeling their hurt. I would not ever, ever return to that because I couldn't trust. The trust is just gone, majorly gone. I mean he is a cheat. He is a liar.

The breaching of trust, the sense of betrayal, the hurt caused by the lies and denials involved in the infidelity are the antithesis of showing love and care. The women described how they hated having to search for evidence in a bid to find out what had been going on but they could no longer trust their husbands to tell the truth. Some of the women had their suspicions for a while and went searching for proof; searching drawers, pockets, mobile phones and emails. Others, like Irene, had no clue. Disclosure came as a huge shock.

Other Reasons for Separating

Kay's situation is somewhat different from the others in that her husband initiated separation but it was not because he was having an affair. Kay's husband was attending counselling in relation to issues from his childhood. In the course of the counselling he made a decision that he needed time and space for himself away from his wife and children.

> KAY: Brian literally came in in April, he didn't leave until July, he came in in April and sat down, and that's when he said that he needed to go away and get some work on himself, and it was all to do with counselling ... And this came to me out of nowhere, it had never been mentioned before ... and the next morning he came down and he said, 'ok, so how do we go about a separation?' and I kind of said that separation had never been mentioned, so I thought 'sure we'll see,' or whatever, and I said no more.
>
> L: You thought 'this is a notion he's got, and he'll get over it'?
>
> KAY: Yea, or he'll think about it and realise 'no, this is not what I'm going to do'. He said no more, and the one time we actually had a row was in May or sometime and I gave out because he was saying nothing, and he just literally shrank away to himself. He didn't want to talk about it ... He came home literally two weeks later to say he'd an apartment got, did I want to see it! I said 'no. I don't need to know.' I couldn't really believe that this was happening ...

Kay's shock and inability to grasp that her husband was serious about separating are similar reactions to those described in relation to the men whose wives initiated separation or to the women who suddenly learned about affairs. Non-initiators take time to process what is happening.

The only couple (Mary) who came close to separating by mutual agreement was the couple who had lived abroad for thirteen years and who had gone to counselling. Mary's reaction to her husband's announcement that he was leaving was very different to the other non-initiators in the study.

> MARY: The tension in the house was horrible and it was very difficult for my daughter as well. I was actually working up the courage to ask him to leave. I just thought on it for a while trying to work up my courage and one day he came home and said he felt trapped and he found it very difficult to be here and realised he was fighting all the time with our daughter and he was going to move out. I was like 'oh yay' ha ha ha 'halleluja'. I was like 'wow'.

This couple had lived in a society in which divorce was more common that it was in Ireland. They also lived in a society in which it was not considered abnormal to go to counselling. These factors may have made a difference. Research (Aronson *et al.*, 2003) shows that couples who separate by agreement tend to cope better and to have less acrimonious relationships following separation than couples where separation involves an initiator and a non-initiator.

Explaining the Separation to Others

The women found telling their children and family and friends that they were separating to be one of the most difficult parts of the process.

> HELEN: Now when I finally did tell my parents, it was dreadful. Telling the children and telling my parents were the worst days of my life.
> L: Because that makes it real.
> HELEN: Yes. It really did.

In many cases, there was no agreement between spouses with regard to when to tell people or what to tell them.

> IRENE: I needed time to process what was going on. He didn't allow me that really because he was very quick to tell. As soon as he met somebody, he'd just say out to them 'we're separated. That's it'. I hadn't even told my sisters or anybody 'cos I thought 'I need time to think about this. What's the impact on our lives?' It was the year my daughter was doing her Leaving Cert. and I didn't want to upset that.

As the following examples show, it appeared that each partner explained the reason for the separation differently.

> ANNE: He never acknowledged the upset his drinking was causing to our daughter.
> HELEN: He never acknowledged he was having an affair.
> NORA: He told the children we were not getting on (which was not true). He neglected to tell them he had met another woman.
> KAY: He told his friends the separation was amicable (at a point at which she felt the decision had not really been made).

Again, the differences in how the spouses storied their separations and the manner in which they chose to speak about them reflected the different points each partner was at in the journey of separation. Those who initiated separation were much further along in the process. They had had time to make sense of and justify why separation was the best option for them at this stage of their lives. Those who had only just realised that separation was about to happen needed time to process the news. The same is likely to be true of children. Many of the women felt they were not given the time to process what was happening and they were hurt by the manner in which their separation was represented to others. They were concerned about what people were thinking and saying about them.

Moving Out: Disconnecting

While the statement about wanting to separate often seemed to come 'out of the blue', actually moving out took time which varied from several weeks or months to four years in Breda's case.

> BREDA: We actually lived in the same house for the four years and it was really, really striking because his mother and father had done the same thing ... It took a lot more out of me than it did out of him. One of the things I remember at the time that happened was that Gerry had decided that he was going to Thailand by himself. I said to him, if the marriage means anything, don't go. At that stage, I was far too hurt ... He still went. Despite all his illness, he still travelled there twice each year during the four years we were separating. He met a Thai woman.
> L: How were you at that time?
> BREDA: In bits, absolutely in bits and trying to work as well ... I was angry at him for putting me in the position where I was the one who had to end the marriage because he would not change. I was angry at him for saying I could leave if I wasn't happy.

The women described the period between the time the decision was made and one partner actually moved out as 'particularly harrowing'. Deirdre described it 'as the most difficult of the whole thing'.

> DEIRDRE: It took a whole year, fourteen months in fact, before he actually physically left this house.

L: What was that period like?

DEIRDRE: Very difficult, probably the most difficult of the whole thing.

L: Were you tempted to change your mind?

DEIRDRE: No, I have never, ever felt that I wanted to change my mind. The strain of separating but continuing to live together ... I was still cooking for him. At that stage my daughter was about sixteen. My son was in Dublin but home at the weekends so I was trying to keep things looking normal. How could I say to her when she came home from school 'here's your dinner and we'll sit down and have ours' and then her Dad comes in at half six and he has to get his own dinner? I wouldn't do that to her, it wasn't that I wanted to give him his dinner really. So much of it was about trying to do the right thing to make it easier for them.

There are more separations during boom years than during recessions (O'Hara, 2011). Due to the recession, there may be couples who cannot afford to separate in Ireland at present. This study illustrates how difficult this period can be for everyone concerned. The quotation from Deirdre shows that, even in situations where there is no longer any love, women continue to maintain the *status quo* for the sake of providing a comfortable home atmosphere for their children.

Anne and Eileen, on the other hand, moved out very quickly.

ANNE: So the next day, we packed up our bits and moved into a hotel, three nights and I never went back. That was it. I stayed out ... He didn't know where we were ... and he went on a very bad binge afterwards himself.

L: And how did that make you feel?

ANNE: Well, I just had to cut myself off completely. I couldn't afford to think of anything. I said 'sure I have done everything I can. If anything happens to him, it's not my fault, it's his'. I just cut myself off. I had enough to deal with.

EILEEN: I said that I had found somewhere and he said he was going away and would be back on a certain day and 'be gone'. There was no 'Please don't go, I'm sorry, I love you. It can be different'. There was absolutely nothing. It still didn't register with him.

L: I'm trying to imagine what it must have felt like for you to pack your car and to drive off on you own after twenty six years.

EILEEN: There were no tears. I just got organised. It was literally a question of just walking out. I didn't shed any tears ... because I had lived this life on my own really, even though we lived in the same house, I was so glad to have my own space.

The Pain and the Shame: Initial Reactions

For her doctoral dissertation at the Institute for Clinical Social Work in Chicago, Doris Wineman (1999) held focus groups involving a total of eighteen women who had divorced in midlife. She identified six stages that women tended to go through in their journeys through divorce. She refers to the stage where the separation is actually happening as 'the horror of it all' and uses this phrase to describe the depression, fear, loss, shame and general upset that women felt immediately following separation.

All of the women in this study, both initiators and non-initiators, described 'the horror of it all' and feeling pain and shame at the time of their separations. Helen and Irene outlined their physical and emotional reactions to learning about their husbands' infidelity and their decisions to separate.

> L: We are looking at the events surrounding the separation. Can you remember how you felt when he said 'I'm leaving'?
>
> IRENE: Well I was just overwhelmed really. My heart sank. I got a terrible pain in my chest or in my breast. I don't know where it was. I remember thinking as I was walking down the canal 'Oh my God, the pain'. But I was overwhelmed by the thought that I was betrayed. I remember thinking in my head 'I mustn't react. I mustn't lash out. I need to take on board all what's happening here.' I used to write. I wrote as much down as I possibly could, I was trying to piece things together. I was feeling so hurt. The pain was unbelievable really.

> HELEN: I stayed awake all night and worried, worried, worried and my face showed it, it was very thin. I was gaunt looking. I would sit up. I just couldn't sleep. I'd come downstairs and just didn't know what to do, where to turn, what to do.
>
> L: How much time did you spend crying?
>
> HELEN: Loads. And I had panic attacks because I was just afraid. I was so fearful of the future. I was so fearful. What are we going to do? The girls came first. I don't know how I was getting through days. It was a complete haze, what was going on, trying to keep it from everybody.

Some of the women also described the pain felt by their husbands prior to or at the time of separation. Geraldine described how her husband was hospitalised after spending a night trying 'to figure out how to top himself'.

Nora described her husband getting chest pains and having panic attacks. Both women felt their husbands were struggling with how to tell their wives that they wanted to separate.

> NORA: He said to me: 'I will die.' He used often say: 'I have a pain in my heart.' And I used say 'God, are you getting a heart attack?' because his father got heart attacks, you know. And 'I can't breathe.' And I know at night he would be like that, like getting panic attacks in the middle of the night. And I'd say: 'Go to the doctor and see. What are you stressed over?' I'd say: 'Tell me what's bothering you?' you know. And he'd say: 'Well, there's nothing really bothering me.' But, I suppose this is what was bothering him. This is what was on his mind that he wanted to tell me this, he was leaving but he didn't know how and I think, you know ... He felt trapped.

Anne stated that her husband went on a drinking binge after she left. Sarah described her husband as going into a 'big depression'. Catherine felt her husband had a nervous breakdown.

> SARAH: So I told him and he cried and he went into a big depression and didn't know what to do ... He was broken hearted, just broken hearted, 'breaking up the family, and how could I do it to my children', and all of this, but I was resolved, I was going to die staying in there, I was so trapped and a basket case and you know, 'I can't live like this', the mantra, 'I can't live like this'.

> CATHERINE: Then he moved into an apartment about two miles down the road. He lives very quietly. I have seen him, like I'd say he went through a nervous breakdown ... I met him one evening and I said to him 'you know you are suffering from depression. Go to your doctor.' Now depression is just a nasty word but he did go and the doctor put him on medication.

At the early stages of going through separation, several of the women stated that they were experiencing physical symptoms. They were having trouble sleeping and eating. They were unable to stop crying, had headaches, chest pains and panic attacks. They felt anxious, depressed and generally unwell. Anne and Helen went to see their family doctors but felt that their doctors did not have the time to listen to them and just prescribed sleeping tablets and antidepressants.

L: How about support from your doctor?
ANNE: No support. He knew our situation for years. He has been our family doctor. He was very supportive to my husband and knew about his problem but never once mentioned Al Anon to me.
L: But he prescribed antidepressants and sleeping tablets?
ANNE: That was it. He didn't have a lot of time.

HELEN: I did go to the doctor at another stage ... He spoke to me and he gave me sleeping tablets. I said 'I don't really want them. Take them anyway.' I got them but I never took them. Then he wanted to try and give me valium or something like that. I said 'no' ... He had me crying in the place ... I moved doctors ... But that kind of attitude ... 'give her antidepressants, silly little woman ... '

Catherine and Mary also felt that medication was not the solution they needed at that time.

L: Were you sleeping at that time?
CATHERINE: I took sleeping tablets up until about the week after he had left ... I was only sleeping for three or four hours.
L: Did you go for antidepressants?
CATHERINE: No. I didn't because I felt 'I'm not depressed. I'm grieving and I can't be any other way than what I am'. I didn't go to the doctor.

MARY: I never took medication. I'm not a great sleeper anyway. There were times when I didn't sleep great. I had terrible headaches but I've always had headaches. But I haven't been on any medication.

Family doctors are likely to be amongst the first professionals that women who are recently separated turn to for help. It is important that general practitioners understand the emotional difficulties as well as the physical symptoms which may be manifested during the process of separation.

The pain coming through and the language used by the women in these quotations is similar to the language used by people who experience a trauma or a crisis. Writing about working in a marriage counselling service, O'Connor (2001) describes the level of pain and emotional upset as being similar to the level of trauma in an accident and emergency department of a hospital. Sarah, Deirdre and Eileen all stated that they felt they were going to die if they stayed living with their husbands. Their level of pain was that acute.

The event of separating as described by these women meets the criteria Parad and Parad (2005) identify as constituting a crisis:

> There is (1) a specific and identifiable precipitating event, (2) the event is perceived as meaningful and threatening, (3) disorganisation or disequilibrium result from the stressful event and (4) the coping and interventive tasks involved in resolving the problem may be adaptive or maladaptive (p. 5).

Discovering infidelity and hearing about the initiator's intention to leave are the events that precipitate a crisis. All of the women described separation as being meaningful in the sense that it was the end of a marriage which had been an important part of their lives. Initially the non-initiators, in particular, felt that their futures were threatened and that their homes and their children were in jeopardy. They responded by crying constantly, having panic attacks, experiencing physical pain, being unable to sleep or eat, being disoriented and feeling overwhelmed by both physical and emotional pain. One woman described how she had attempted suicide. She had been out with friends and when she dropped them home and they each went into their houses to be with their husbands, she could not cope with going into her own house knowing that her husband was never coming back. She described how she was overcome with loneliness and that her 'heart was broken'.

Clinicians (Scuka, 2015) working with couples following infidelity often use a 'trauma model' (p. 145) of treatment. This is 'a model for understanding the subjective experience of infidelity as akin to the experience of trauma' (p. 145). A trauma-like response can lead to a grief-like response. The language the women used is also the language of loss and grief. Worden's (1991) first two tasks of grieving, to accept the reality of the loss and to work through the pain, seem particularly relevant for what the women felt they needed to do in order to cope with the trauma of separation. They needed to accept the reality of the separation, that there was no way back and they needed to deal with the pain and try to keep functioning.

As well as describing the pain they felt, several of the women described feeling ashamed. They had just discovered that their husbands were cheating on them, yet the women were the ones feeling ashamed.

L: How was it your failure?

HELEN: I don't even know how to explain it. I did feel a failure and I still feel ashamed, partly. And then I felt for the children that they were coming from a 'broken home' and that stigma, I suppose. Even though I know it's … not like that now.

L: Do you think that still exists?

HELEN: No, it doesn't and I know there's so much of it (separation) but there's just something there, you know. Failure I think it was.

L: What's the shame about?

IRENE: I presume because the person I have chosen in life as part of my family, I got it so wrong, maybe. My sadness is for my kids that now this is changing our history forever. They are now from what they call a 'broken home' and I knew they'd be so hurt. I suppose I felt some responsibility really as well. I felt so alone at the time … The first year was just so difficult really … Of course I was angry. Of course I was in disbelief.

Several of the women talked about feeling shame and a sense of failure and worrying that their 'failure' would be reflected upon their children. Bateson (1989) wrote about how separation is often seen as a failure to 'succeed' in a relationship. It may involve failure to choose the right person or failure to make the relationship work. Both involve mistakes (Bateson, 1989). The sense of failure was felt not only by the initiators of the separations but also by the non-initiators. The women felt that they did not 'fit' into society anymore and that they had lost their identity and their status. While they had not been made to feel like outcasts, they still felt ashamed and embarrassed.

The women's description of shame is similar to a finding by van Schalkwyk (2005) in a South African study. The women in South Africa described how their previous construction of themselves as relational beings was largely lost following divorce and how they felt responsible for the failure of their relationships. One woman in the South African study described the process of disengaging from her relationship with her husband as being like 'the live amputation of a limb' (p. 94).

For the women in this study, their sense of shame came, not so much from how they were treated by others as, from within themselves. The beliefs about marriage and the attitudes to separation that they had internalised as children came back to haunt them. There were several references to 'broken homes' and to the stigma their children would be subject to as a result of coming from a 'broken home'. Like the women in the South African study and the women in McDaniel and Coleman's study in Missouri (2003) the women in this study also blamed themselves for the failure of their marriages. The women in each study felt they were expected to oversee the creation of 'happy families', an essential part of which involved keeping their husbands and their children happy and that somehow they had failed to do this.

Initial Reactions of Children

All of the children whose mothers were involved in this study were in their teenage or young adult years when their parents separated. Their reactions to news of their parents' separations varied. Anne and Deirdre said that their children were not surprised. Deirdre mentioned how hard she found it to talk to the children about her reasons for wanting to separate and how she regrets not having been able to give her children more opportunities to say how they were feeling. Both women appear to have found it particularly difficult to talk to their sons.

> ANNE: They both said neither of them were shocked. My daughter was happy to be out of the situation. My son said 'Ma, I know things weren't going right. Sure I'm not a bit surprised. It doesn't bother me' (You know what fellas are like). 'I'm going to be up and gone in a few more years anyway so it won't matter'. But, actually, he didn't stay in college then. He came back at that time and he went to live at home with his Da. I would say that he felt because we had gone that he had a duty to stay with him.

> DEIRDRE: Their reaction was 'we knew things weren't right anyway'. There was no great surprise. I have to say I found it very hard to talk to them about it. We didn't talk. That is something I feel bad about, maybe I should have given them more opportunities to say how they were feeling. I couldn't, I was just trying to hold myself together on the outside for them. I probably didn't really know what to say to them.

Breda also referred to not talking much to her son about how he felt about her decision to separate from his Dad.

L: How did he react to your decision?

BREDA: It's difficult to tell ... Again this is a repeat of a pattern. When my husband's parents were separating, he said he would not take sides. My son did exactly the same.

L: How do you think your daughter was affected by the separation?

BREDA: She was very upset to leave her father and her home. She needs a very stable environment ... There was a lot of change. We went from being four to being two.

Frances also said that her children were not surprised and were very matter-of-fact about the news.

FRANCES: Well my children have a very matter of fact kind of approach ... My eldest daughter felt 'it's not a bad thing that you're separating because it's not very nice'. My younger daughter would be the same. 'You're not getting on, so why would you live together?'

L: So they were aware that you weren't getting on?

FRANCES: Absolutely. We had a family meeting one time and Sean had moved out for three weeks at this stage and he wanted to come back. So we had a family meeting to see what the rest of the children felt. I remember Karly looking Sean straight in the face and she said 'I love you daddy but I don't want you back. There's too much upset in the house. Mam is far happier when you're not here.'

In other situations where mothers had initiated separations, children were very upset. Eileen and Sarah explain how negative their children were towards them initially.

EILEEN: My children were very, very upset, very, very upset. It has taken them over a year to come around ... I wasn't happy, I wanted out but I didn't have the courage to do it. And then when I did get the courage, I was gone. I was out the door within six/seven weeks of saying 'I want a break' ...

L: Did the girls blame you for breaking up the family?

SARAH: Yes, the second one particularly took it very, very badly that I abandoned her at age twenty. The other two understood. They didn't like it, and the older girl ... was surprised at how shocked she was, even though she knew it was a possibility, the fact of it being a fact that now her two parents were going to separate, not being the family home, was going to be changed ...

In situations where separations were as a result of a father's infidelity, most children were very angry at their fathers and very upset.

IRENE: Well, initially, they were very cross with him really. They were angry at him ...

NORA: The youngest girl, went anorexic and she didn't speak to her father for nearly a year.
L: Did you think she didn't forgive him for having the affair?
NORA: She didn't. No. She didn't forgive him. She didn't. 'How could he do this to us?'

Helen and Jane had children who were away studying when news of the separation broke. This added a further dimension to telling their children and to their children's reactions.

HELEN: So then he said he was going to tell the other two here. Then he paid for a flight for the other girl to come home and I'll never forget meeting her at the airport. She came in all delighted that she was home and then we needed to talk to her that night ... She was devastated because she hadn't been around.

JANE: They were all starting to go just before this. Sarah was gone away when it happened, and Emily was in London, so Anne lived through it all that weekend. She was here, witnessing, so she's the problem, she's the angriest ...

Children's reactions to their parents' separations varied. For children who had witnessed fights and arguments between their parents, the news did not come as a big surprise. However, in households where there had been very little overt conflict, where mothers had not told anyone how unhappy they were or where fathers' affairs were suddenly disclosed or discovered, the unexpected nature of the separations caused serious distress to the children. In stressful situations where children could normally rely on their parents to support them, many of the mothers were not in a position to be supportive. Mothers were struggling to cope with their own decisions and emotions and it hurt even more to see how their children were also struggling. From the accounts given by the women, fathers would also seem to have been stressed and unable to be supportive to their children around the time of separation.

Transition and Loss

Because women at midlife are likely to be leaving long-term relationships, separation/divorce at this stage involves more significant losses and changes in relationships, routines and roles than for younger women. By midlife, patterns established during marriage may have been in existence for decades (Sakraida, 2005). This was the case for the women in this study. The shortest marriage amongst the fourteen women was twenty years (Geraldine) and the longest was thirty-five years (Catherine). Most of the women had known their husbands for over half of their life spans. Some of them had met in their teens and had never been with another man. To separate was for them a crisis.

Coming to terms with all the losses involved in separating requires a period of mourning (Carter and McGoldrick, 2005). Practitioners (Fisher and Alberti, 2006) who work with people following separation base much of their work on the stages of mourning (Kubler-Ross, 1997). Feelings of shock, denial, anger and depression need to be worked through before a person arrives at acceptance and begins to adapt to the situation. Those who initiate separation seem to have done the equivalent of 'anticipatory grief work' prior to separating. They describe how they 'cried it out for years beforehand and that separation was just tying it off because it had died already' (Sarah). For the non-initiators, women, men and children, separation can appear to happen unexpectedly and traumatically and require a far longer period of adjustment.

According to the women in this study, a key difference between coping with death and coping with separation is the shame and betrayal that they felt about separation. There are also differences in how support is provided or is not provided, as is the more common scenario. Nobody in the study, neither initiators nor non-initiators, wanted or expected their marriages to end in separation. Nobody in the families concerned found it easy to separate.

Legal, Financial and Housing Arrangements

This chapter will continue to explore the third research question about the losses and gains experienced on the journey through separation. It will deal with experiences of the family law system and the legal arrangements the women made about their accommodation and income following separation. The chapter will, firstly, outline the background to divorce and separation legislation in Ireland. The chapter will also discuss experiences of mediation services, the significance of having older children, feelings associated with staying in or leaving family homes and income and pension arrangements.

Background to Divorce Referendum 1986

While this study is primarily concerned with separation, attitudes to marital breakdown in Ireland were seen most clearly in the debates that surrounded the two referenda on divorce in 1986 and 1995. Divorce had not always been illegal in Ireland. The ban was introduced in the 1937 Constitution which stated that 'No law shall be enacted providing for the dissolution of marriage' (Article 41.3.1). Having no divorce in Ireland was part of a vision of what it was to be Irish, as opposed to English, and what it was to be Catholic rather than Protestant. It was part of Eamon de Valera's (Prime Minister) vision of an independent Catholic Ireland. It took almost fifty years for the reality of marriage breakdown to be acknowledged and for the need for divorce to be debated publicly (Hill, 2003).

The first public acknowledgement of the need to legislate for divorce in Ireland was the establishment by the government of the Joint Committee on Marriage Breakdown in 1984. The Committee's Report (1985) stated that:

> what motivated the Oireachtas[1] to establish the Committee was firstly the need to protect family life and secondly a growing awareness of marriage breakdown as a social reality, giving rise to social, economic and legal problems which required detailed examination and intervention by the State, if necessary, by legal or constitutional means (p. 27).

It was in keeping with the policy at the time that protecting family life was mentioned as the primary objective of the Committee. The Committee acknowledged that there were 'many thousands of couples who find themselves in a legal limbo – tied into a marriage that in social reality no longer exists' (1985: 29). The Committee recommended that a referendum be held to amend the Constitution. It suggested that a form of 'no fault' divorce, which would avoid some of the worst impacts of divorce found in other countries, be put to the electorate for their consideration. The first referendum to amend the Constitution and legalise divorce was announced by the Taoiseach (Prime Minister), Garret Fitzgerald on 23rd April 1986.

Initial polls showed support for the amendment and that a majority of people were prepared to consider the possibility of legalising divorce (Whelan and Fahey, 1994) but as the campaign progressed it became clear that support was dropping (Dillon, 1993; Burley and Regan, 2002). The main opposition to divorce was led by a group called the Anti-Divorce Group. This was a group of Catholic lay people (as opposed to clergy) which only formed after the referendum was announced. The primary spokesman for the group was William Binchy, a well-known barrister. The Catholic hierarchy did not take part in the campaign at an official level although some individual bishops and priests addressed the matter in Episcopal letters and in sermons at Sunday Masses (Dillon, 1993; Hill, 2003).

The argument advanced by people in the 'No' campaign was that no human authority could change what God had ordained. 'What God

---

1   The parliament of Ireland.

has joined together, let no man put asunder'. Marriage was seen, first and foremost, as a sacrament, with God at its centre. Marriage was perceived as being sacred and not just a civil contract which could be entered into and dissolved according to the laws of the State. Marriage was seen as the basis of the family, which was, in turn, seen as the basis of social order in society. The fear expressed was that divorce would undermine the stability of the family which Irish people, as per their Constitution, held to be sacred. Binchy (1984) stated that 'the availability of divorce would tend to increase the demand for it and contribute to the lessening of efforts to find alternative solutions' (p. 8). The fear was that divorce would destabilise marriages and that couples would not put sufficient effort into trying to resolve marital difficulties if divorce were an option.

The 'No' campaigners did not deny that couples separated, but their contention was that divorce would benefit a second family at the expense of a first family. Research findings from other countries were presented to support this argument (Binchy, 1984). The concern was that women and children of the first relationship would not be financially provided for as a result of divorce and that they would lose their inheritance rights. As in most debates, the 'No' campaigners were not entirely wrong (Burley and Regan, 2002). The legal situation at the time meant that rural women would have had no entitlement to the family farm in the event of divorce. It was suggested that before women would vote for divorce, property law reforms would have to be enacted (Dillon, 1993). These changes were made before the subsequent divorce referendum in 1995.

As it transpired, the 1986 Referendum on Divorce was rejected by 64% of the electorate. The referendum results show a very strong rural vote in opposition to the introduction of divorce. Concern about financial security for women and about their legal entitlement to land were some of the issues which resulted in the majority of Irish people voting 'no' to divorce in 1986. The explanation put forward for the 'no' vote was that while Ireland had modernised economically in the 1960s and 1970s, in the moral domain it still resembled a more traditional conservative society (Hill, 2003). Legalising divorce 'would penetrate directly the bedrock of Irish values' (Dillon, 1993: 30) and in 1986 Irish people were not ready to make the transition from traditional, conservative 'family' values to more liberal values.

The Judicial Separation and Family Law Act, 1989

The Government still had to deal with the ambiguous position of the many people who were separated but had no access to any legal arrangements to regularise their situations. In 1989, the Judicial Separation and Family Law Act which enabled couples to separate legally, but not to re-marry, was introduced. This legislation is still in use and is often the first legal remedy which couples in Ireland utilise to legalise their affairs following separation (Coulter, 2008; Mahon and Moore, 2011).

The grounds for a Judicial Separation are as follows:

- adultery by the respondent
- desertion for at least one year
- behaviour with which the applicant cannot reasonably be expected to live
- spouses have lived apart for one year, if they both agree to the separation and for three years, if there is not agreement to separate
- the marriage is broken down to the degree that satisfies the Court
- a normal marriage relationship between the spouses has not existed for at least a year (Shatter, 1997).

The grounds most often cited are that the relationship has broken down irretrievably.

Financial protection for women and children, in the form of maintenance payments, are covered under this Act. The Court also must be satisfied that the religious, physical, social, moral and intellectual welfare of children are provided for on a permanent basis before a Separation Order is issued. This Act has been described as 'a limited form of back door divorce' (Burley and Regan, 2002:205) in that it contained many of the provisions of divorce legislation in other countries. There seems to have been very little opposition to this legislation when it was going through the Dáil (Whelan and Fahey, 1994). The weaknesses in Act were that it involved long delays for many applicants and it was very expensive (Burley and Regan, 2002).

The expectation was that once divorce was introduced in 1997, the legislation on separation would be used less often (Coulter, 2008). This has not transpired. Rather than waiting the required four years before applying for divorce, many Irish couples apply for a separation, which can be done after just one year. The arrangements made under judicial separation legislation often then become a blueprint for subsequent divorce settlements and amount to a two-step legal process in how divorce is handled in Ireland (Coulter, 2008).

Second Referendum on Divorce 1995

In 1992 the Government produced a *White Paper on Marital Breakdown*. It estimated that the number of separated couples had doubled since 1986 and that the number of women claiming Deserted Wives benefits had trebled. There was pressure on the government from groups representing separated people to hold another referendum on divorce. In order to get all-party agreement before attempting to hold another referendum, some of the concerns raised in the first referendum about the financial situation of the 'first' family were addressed and the grounds on which divorce could be obtained were made 'extremely restrictive' (Burley and Regan, 2002: 207).

In November 1995, the second referendum on divorce was held. The reality of judicial separation had been accepted by the enactment of the 1989 Act and the government argued for divorce on the mainly pragmatic grounds that so many people were already separated and in second relationships and that their situations needed to be legalised. Assurances were given that any divorce legislation introduced would ensure that proper provision was made for the women and children in 'first' families. By November 1995 when the second referendum on divorce took place, Ireland was a very different place than it had been in 1986. There were more single mothers, more women in the workforce, more women in third level education and religious observance had dropped (Coulter, 1997). There had also been a number of high profile scandals involving clergymen in the intervening decade. A different attitude to the Catholic Church, and to following the rules laid down by the Catholic Church, prevailed partly because of these clerical scandals (Ferriter, 2009).

Notwithstanding the changes that had taken place in Irish society in the intervening years, heated debates again took place, as in 1986, during the referendum campaign. 'A campaign of fear' (Burley and Regan, 2002: 207) was again launched in opposition to divorce. Hill (2003) stated that 'the anti-divorce groups warned that the 'individualism' of feminists and other liberals represented a real threat to Irish morality' (p. 190). Anti-Divorce Campaign posters read 'hello divorce ... bye bye Daddy'. They appear to have been suggesting that fathers would leave their wives and children if they were given the choice to divorce and re-marry.

The referendum to amend the constitutional ban on divorce was passed with only 50.28% voting in favour of divorce. This was the smallest majority that any amendment has ever been passed by in the State (Mc Gréil, 1997: 31; Considine and Dukelow, 2009: 71). The turnout of voters was 61.94 %. The referendum result was challenged in the High Court and in the Supreme Court which caused a delay of a further fifteen months before divorce legislation was finally passed.

The Family Law (Divorce) Act (1996) finally came into operation in February 1997. The four grounds on which divorce can be granted under the Act include:

- that a couple have lived apart for four of the previous five years
- that there is no prospect of a reconciliation
- that provision is made for the spouses and children
- that any further conditions imposed by the Court are complied with (Shatter, 1997; Nestor, 2006).

The tiny majority in favour of legalising divorce indicates that in 1995 there was still a sizeable minority of people in Ireland who were against removing the ban on divorce. There was also a clear rural-urban split in how votes were cast, with a majority of voters in rural areas firmly in opposition to divorce (Burley and Regan, 2002). The campaigns that were run in opposition to the two referenda on divorce illustrate the depth of feeling and fear about marriage breakdown and divorce in Ireland that were felt by many people less than twenty years ago.

At the same time, there were some high profile examples of separated people in public life, such as Conor Cruise O'Brien who had been a government Minister and Bertie Ahern who was the Taoiseach (Prime Minister). Their separated status did not appear to be an issue. It was accepted that Mr Ahern was in a new relationship and was accompanied by his partner on formal State occasions. Yet for 'ordinary', 'respectable' people separation was an issue, as evidenced by the numbers who voted against divorce. This slightly paradoxical situation, whereby to be separated/divorced was to be a 'failure' on the one hand, while on the other hand, the separated status of some high profile people was unremarkable, is the backdrop against which the women in this study separated. Table 3 presents a summary of their situations.

Table 3: Legal, Financial and Housing Arrangements

Name	Length Separated	Mediation/ Separation/ Divorce	Current Ages of Children	Housing Wife	Maintenance Wife/ Children	Income
Anne	2 years	Mediation failed – separation pending	1 under 18 1 over 18	Private rental + 1 child	Nil	Professional
Breda	7	Divorced	2 over 18 1 with special needs	Private rental + 1 child	Nil	Carer
Catherine	1	No proceedings	3 over 18 left home	Family home	Nil	Professional
Deirdre	5	Separation agreed in mediation	1 student 1 abroad	Family home – she bought him out. Mortgage until 70	Education costs shared	Professional
Eileen	1	Mediation failed – divorce proceedings initiated	3 left home 2 still students	Private rental	Wife's rent paid	Professional
Frances	5	Mediation failed – judicial separation	3 adults (1 mother and child with wife)	New house Mortgage until 70	Nil	Professional
Geraldine	5	Mediation failed – divorced	3 children in Third level	Family home until 2017	500 euro per month	Clerical worker

Name	Length Separated	Mediation/ Separation/ Divorce	Current Ages of Children	Housing Wife	Maintenance Wife/ Children	Income
Helen	4	Mediation failed – divorce pending	2 in Third level 1 graduate abroad	Family home	Nil	P/t Clerical worker
Irene	2	Mediation pending	3 in Third Level	Rented family home	Nil	Professional
Jane	2	Judicial separation pending	1 in Third level 2 working	Family home No settlement yet	100 euro p/w to wife + college costs	P/t shop assistant
Kay	6	Mediation failed – divorced	1 in Third level 1 working abroad	Family home	Nil	Professional
Sarah	4	Separation agreed in mediation	2 in Third level 1 working	She bought a new house Mortgage until 69	Education costs shared	Professional
Mary	2	Separation/ divorce agreed	1 child in secondary school	Family home with child until she reaches 18	Lump sum	Student (ex-executive)
Nora	1	No proceedings	1 in Third level 1 working	Family home for sale	bills shared	P/t shop assistant

Initiating Legal Proceedings: Public Ending

One of the difficulties discussed by Coulter (2008) and Lunn *et al.* (2009) in gathering statistics on the prevalence of separation is that the figures emanating from Court applications for Judicial Separation and Divorce do not tally with the number of women who report themselves to be separated in the census returns in Ireland. The suggestion made is that some couples separate but do not legally formalise the separation. As can be seen from Table 3, three of the women (Catherine, Irene and Nora) are in this position.

> CATHERINE: I haven't gone there. We have no separation agreement. I have spoken to my solicitor, a lovely, lovely woman. I've seen her three times and she didn't charge me. She's unbelievable. I'll leave it be for the moment ... I didn't want to do it, head in the sand stuff. I'm not sure.

> L: What sort of arrangements have you come to, so far?
> NORA: None. He went to the solicitor first and I think it wasn't really a separation. What we wanted was to write down an agreement about what he would pay and what I would pay. Now unfortunately, our solicitor died. But no, we've left it and I'm not forcing the issue of a separation.

Table 3 shows that these two women were separated for less than two years. Both of them had been through previous periods of separation followed by periods of reconciliation. The third woman (Irene) talked about only being ready two years after she separated, to even start the mediation process.

> IRENE: Well I did go to a solicitor for some advice and she said to me to go to the court and get an Order but when it came to the time of going to the court, I didn't have the courage to go into a court ... Two years on, it's now time for me to do something about this. So I registered with the mediation service ...

Time and emotional strength seem to be factors in readiness to initiate legal proceedings. Going to a solicitor and going to court make separation public and a legal reality. Speaking to a solicitor moves personal and previously secret relationship difficulties into a public domain. It involves 'washing dirty linen' in public. It takes some people time to accept that reconciliation is not going to happen and that the separation is final. It takes emotional strength to begin to deal with the practicalities and legal formalities involved in separating. It signals the official fragmenting of a marital relationship and time is needed to process the loss of lifestyle and identity at an emotional level.

One of the grounds on which divorce can be granted in Ireland under the Family Law (Divorce) Act (1996) is that a couple have lived apart for four of the previous five years (Nestor, 2006). Seven of the fourteen women in the study had been separated for three years or less at the time of their interviews. Three (Catherine, Irene, Nora) had not initiated legal proceedings. Three women (Anne, Eileen, Jane) were in the process of getting judicial separations/divorces. Five (Deirdre, Frances, Helen, Sarah, Mary) had separation agreements/judicial separations. Three (Breda, Geraldine, Kay) were divorced. This mirrors what Lunn *et al.* (2009) describe as 'a patchwork of legal remedies, from *de facto* and legal separations to full divorce' (p. 57).

Ireland is unusual in an international context in having such a two-stage legal approach to the dissolution of marriage. The expectation when divorce was introduced was that judicial separation would no longer be required (Coulter, 2008). Coulter suggests that the reason so many Irish women initiate proceedings for judicial separations is because they cannot wait four years to have arrangements made about ownership of the family home, about custody, access and maintenance of children. If couples are in agreement, they can initiate proceedings for a judicial separation after only one year.

Most of the children in the families surveyed were older teenagers at the time of their parents' separation so custody and access were not an issue. Ownership of the family home, payment of household bills and maintenance of young adults who were in third-level education were, however, seen as urgent issues that the women in this study needed to address sooner than the four years required to proceed to divorce, hence their decisions to apply for judicial separations.

L: Are things all sorted out legally?
FRANCES: Oh, they were all sorted out legally on the day we separated ...

L: Do you think you will get a divorce?

FRANCES: I used to think 'well, a divorce is final' and I don't know whether I want that. Having said that, being separated is like being in no man's land. It is neither one thing nor the other. So I don't know. I honestly don't know ...

L: It's just an unusual thing in an international context that some Irish people separate and don't proceed to divorce.

FRANCES: I suppose it's a recent thing and I suppose I really don't know.

L: And it's not on religious grounds, because divorce is a sin?

FRANCES: Ah, no.

The stipulation that couples be separated for four of the previous five years before applying for a divorce did not emerge in this study as a major concern. Only one of the women (Mary) felt that it might be an issue for younger women who might wish to have children with a new partner. Some of the women also referred to a desire 'to move on with their lives' as being part of their motivation for applying for judicial separations or divorce. Going to court signified an attempt, not only on a practical level but also on an emotional level, to get some degree of closure, to begin to plan for the future, to forge a new identity and to make a new beginning.

HELEN: I know it's going to be very, very, very tough but I'm ready for it. I haven't even got a proper separation agreement but I'm going for divorce now ... I wouldn't have thought of divorce initially but for my own future and to secure myself financially, I want to get rid of him financially. I know he's in a lot of debt and I'm afraid he'll come back to me looking for more money. I have spoken about this to my parents ... Both of them were in agreement 'get rid of him. Go for it.' And both of them would be quite religious as well.

L: Tie up your loose ends.

HELEN: Yes and be able to move on because always in the back of my mind ... I'm recording everything, everything I spend ... And it just wears you down and I want that gone.

As with almost all aspects of this study, the women had varying experiences in their dealings with the legal system. Kay had some interesting points to make:

L: You were saying that the legal system is a 'dense forest'?

KAY: I felt totally abused by the solicitor in terms of cost and in terms of attention. I was quoted one price and the final bill presented was another ... No breakdown on the bill just for 'services rendered'. I felt that I was in a major position of distress, and I think you are just seen as someone to make some money out of. No great property and it wasn't a 'sexy' case so let's just shove it through the system and see what we get.

L: So your problem really was with your own solicitor?

KAY: Yes ... but anytime you go anywhere to ask for advice, everyone has conflicting advice. Nobody seems to know how the system works. Nobody will tell you 'well this is your situation so ABCD will follow. Even the solicitors on the day were saying 'oh, this is a new judge and we don't want to try him now and this is a comment he made yesterday' and it seemed terribly personalised, and it was down to how good a humour was he in after his breakfast this morning! It's so arbitrary.

Kay is making the point that she found it difficult to make important legal arrangements about her home and her future income while she was still in a fragile emotional state. Her stress was increased by a lack of clarity in the legal advice she received and a lack of transparency in the billing arrangements.

Negotiating Endings: Experiences of Mediation

Solicitors are obliged to tell separating couples about the existence of the Family Mediation Service but attendance at mediation is voluntary. The Family Mediation Service currently operates as part of the Legal Aid Board. It is a state-run service which employs professionally qualified mediators and has full-time offices in 5 locations in Dublin, as well as offices in Cork, Galway and Limerick. There are part-time offices located in 9 other locations around the country (<www.legalaidboard>). The service is provided free of charge. Erwin (2007) drew attention to the low uptake of mediation in 2006, quoting figures which showed that only 1,500 couples accessed mediation out of the 27,000 who went to the District and Circuit Courts. According to Conneely (2002), half the couples who attended mediation succeeded in reaching agreements. A much lower proportion of the women in this study managed to reach agreements through mediation. Of the eight women in this study who used the service, only two succeeded in reaching an agreement.

> DEIRDRE: The mediation was absolutely fantastic. I mean he was very co-operative in that. It made the whole thing very straightforward to have somebody else there to help us sort it out. I got the house valued. I bought him out of the house. I had to take out a boosted mortgage on top of taking over the balance of the mortgage. He had to get another mortgage as well ...

Sarah did not have such a positive experience of mediation but they still managed to come to an agreement.

> SARAH: It got very nasty in the mediation. He kind of had broken down ... You'd think he wasn't an organised person but, by golly when it came to money, he had every penny. It was very hard listening to that, you know, and I said, 'what about all the years I spent minding the children, rearing them, summers minding your mother ... does that count for nothing?' And he said: 'well this is your decision, this is your decision. You're the one instigating. It's not what I want.' But I was strong enough by then to know 'ok, the door is open, I can get out, and I have to go'.

Sarah explained that because she and her husband both worked in the public sector, theirs was not a difficult situation to come to an agreement on.

> SARAH: We went to her (the mediator) and she was lovely, and we worked through it again with her, and it was not a difficult one really because we were both working. Our children are, you know, pretty well done for, there was no access, so it was quite a straightforward as one can be.

Moore (2010) interviewed thirty-nine people who had separated and devised a typology of separating couples which she termed (1) egalitarians (2) involved but constrained parents (3) involved but stressed couples (4) aggrieved parents and (5) excluded fathers (Moore, 2010: 4). She found that 'egalitarians' (p. 135) were more likely to have settled their legal affairs through mediation. She also identified that they were more likely to have been dual-income couples and to have completed third-level education. Sarah and Deirdre fit these criteria in that both they and their husbands worked in the public sector, had very similar salaries and pensions and had completed third-level education. The fact that Sarah and Deirdre identified themselves as the initiators of their separations may also have had a bearing on their success in reaching an agreement. They both wanted out of their marriages and stated that they would have agreed to almost anything.

Mary did not use the mediation service but managed to agree on separation terms in an amicable manner.

> MARY: We had the most amicable separation you can ever imagine. The solicitors couldn't believe it, they said they had never seen anything like it. Since the day he left we haven't fought or had words or anything. So he was very civilised, the most civilised separation. As my solicitor said 'the text book separation. This is how it should be done' because neither of us fought over the small stuff. We didn't fight over our daughter or any of that ... Then of course it turned out he went very quickly into a relationship with a twenty seven year old ...

In Mary's case, it would appear that both parties wanted to separate and there were more than adequate means to provide good lifestyles for both parties into the future.

The stories the other women told about their experiences in mediation were very different from the positive experiences described by Deirdre, Sarah and Mary.

> ANNE: We had nine sessions of mediation. Six is normal/average. I bent over backwards to try to settle things over our house, that's what we have to settle, and I felt I went to the very limit and as far as I could go on that, and he just wasn't prepared to go there, to meet me at all. He was pushing, pushing, pushing for me to accept minimum all the time. So since mediation I have had no contact with him.

Frances described how they attended three sessions of mediation but that her husband felt the female mediator was biased against him and would not go back.

> FRANCES: We did go to mediation at some stage in order to sort out how things were going to split. On the third occasion Sean felt that the female facilitator was having a go at him, that she wasn't exactly neutral and that she was pointing everything he wasn't doing that he should be doing. That was it.

Kay had also tried to use the mediation service. She felt her husband's solicitor was influencing him not to engage with the mediation process.

> KAY: We went to family mediation service and that seemed good. I suggested it, we went, and at the time we decided we'd come back ... six months later maybe ... I can't remember why we postponed it but anyway we did. We went back and he had been to see a solicitor in the meantime, and the whole tone was changed ...
> L: Did you hammer out the agreement in mediation?
> KAY: That failed because his solicitor wanted to fight, his solicitor was very aggressive, very aggressive.

Helen started mediation prior to her husband moving out and described it as a 'disaster'. She talked at length about how hurt she was during the whole mediation process.

> HELEN: I was in the waiting room and he came in and completely ignored me. Then he marched into the room with his suit on him, with his laptop and said 'Oh hello, how are you' to the man and the woman mediators. That man just came down so hard on me. I still think I'm going to do something about it even a few years later. It still bothers me how he treated me. We started off on basic stuff like salaries that you can't lie about and how much it's costing for this, this and this. Then he started bringing in 'she's stopping me from seeing the children.' He started making up lies then about things that I had said on the phone and everything like that. I walked out afterwards and said 'I can't go back to that again'. I was an absolute wreck.

Geraldine also described how powerless she felt during the mediation meetings.

> GERALDINE: We started this mediation process and I was reading those leaflets and I was very upset about it. We started the process and it was going ok. I actually didn't rate the mediator but he rated her even less. If he got stroppy at me (I was completely dominated by him at this stage), you know, if he got into a strop about something, she usually went his way. And I remember ringing her and telling her this. She was very defensive and said 'I don't and I'm not'. And whatever way he wanted it that's the way she said we should do it. I just agreed because I just couldn't argue anymore. (This case was subsequently settled in Court.)

Jane is one of the many thousands of people separating who did not even try to use the mediation service. She felt it would not work in her case because her husband was self-employed and she no longer trusted him to tell the truth about his income.

> L: Did you try to go for mediation?
> JANE: I couldn't because ... he wasn't truthful from the start. He lied to me from the start, about everything. No, no, about the situation. I still don't know why my husband really left me. So how could I trust him?

What seems to be emerging from the stories about failed attempts at mediation is how difficult it can be for couples who are going through a separation to even sit in the same room as each other and negotiate calmly about ownership of a family home and payment of household bills. Even the presence of a neutral mediator does not guarantee that meetings will be conducted in a calm and reasoned manner. It appears that feelings about the events leading to the separation and problems during the marriage are not easily put to one side. Moore (2010) and Mahon and Moore (2011), when writing about their studies on post-separation parenting, came to a similar conclusion. Their conclusion was that patterns established during marriage continued into post-separation relationships. Couples who had been unable to communicate on a deep level during their marriage were unlikely to be able to change their communication style dramatically post-separation.

Another aspect apparent in these extracts is the gendered nature of how negotiations were conducted during mediation. Anne mentioned how she felt pressurised by her husband to accept far less than she felt was equitable. Both Helen and Geraldine felt that their husbands were given far more credence than they were during the mediation process. (Frances's husband felt the opposite because the mediator was asking him to take some responsibility for financial matters that he was not prepared to deal with and did not want to hear about.) While mediators may try to adopt a neutral position in negotiations, the women in this study still felt at a disadvantage and that their husbands held a dominant position.

The timing of mediation and the need for counselling before attending mediation would appear to be important factors in whether mediation is likely to succeed or not. Discussion in the previous section on separation as a series of losses which take time to mourn means that people are likely

to be in a very fragile state at the time at which they need to make important decisions about their homes, themselves and their children. For many
of the women, things said by their husbands during mediation meetings
led to them having no subsequent communication with their husbands.
Rather than mediation resulting in agreement, it was the arena in which
disagreements became even clearer and conflicts more entrenched.

Significance of the Ages of Children

The reason given by both men and women in the *American Active Retirement*
study (Montenegro *et al.*, 2004) for delaying separation until midlife was
because of the perceived negative effect it would have on children. This
was also a consideration for the women who initiated separation in this
study. As previously explained by Deirdre (p. 85), children constitute the
main connecting threads in an otherwise fragmenting relationship and
their children's welfare was a primary consideration for all the women.

> DEIRDRE: I hung on with the children in mind for a long time. When I came to
> the conclusion that this was not going to fix itself, it was probably maybe three/four
> years before I actually did it. There was either one of them doing their Leaving Cert.
> or one of them was moving into college or there seemed to be always some reason
> why this was not a good year. Whether that was me putting it off or out of genuine
> concern for them, I don't know ...

Eileen waited twenty-three years because she thought separating would
be bad for her children.

> EILEEN: I did think of leaving him and I had planned what I was going to do, where
> I was going to live and get a job etc. but at the time, in the 1980s, there was a lot of
> talk about divorce being bad for children and that they were better with both parents.
> I was taking that on board ...

Of the four women who left their family homes, Anne and Breda took
their daughters with them, Sarah's daughter stayed at home to finish her

Leaving Certificate and Eileen waited until her three children had left home before leaving.

Only Mary had a child under seventeen at the time of the interviews. Some children had already left home or were in the process of leaving home at the time of their parents' separations. Weston and Smyth (2000) in their Australian study on the financial consequences of separation for women found that women who separated after the age of forty-five were the most disadvantaged because most of them were found to be either living alone or as single parents. Women living alone into old age could have financial and care implications both for their families and for the State, as well as being a source of serious concern about the future for the women themselves. Some of the women experienced the 'empty nest' syndrome at around the same time as the loss of their husbands as most of their children were in their late teens at the time of the separation. A series of major losses came together in these women's lives.

> DEIRDRE: A year and a half after my husband left I knew that my daughter was going to be leaving home in September and I was going to be on my own. The build-up to that and the thought of that ... I couldn't eat. I couldn't sleep. I was in bits.

Some of the women described their children leaving home as a greater loss than their husbands moving out.

> KAY: My daughter has just moved out this summer. I have said to people I think this will be harder than separation because it's a whole new life.

The majority of the children was still at college and their family home (in which most of their mothers continued to reside) was still very much their home base. Very few of the children were financially self-sufficient. Their mother's domicile still tended to be where adult children gravitated towards. There were clear expenses involved for the mothers in their adult children continuing to spend periods of time at home, yet as will be shown when discussing income and maintenance arrangements, very few of the mothers received any financial support in this regard. Weston and Smyth (2000) found that the presumption in legal settlements that young adults would be financially independent of their parents by the age of twenty-three did not reflect the reality in many families in Australia. They suggested that by the time young people finished education and were able to provide for themselves financially many of them were aged around twenty-seven years of age rather than twenty-three. For some of the women in this study, this finding reflects their situation. Several of the children had gone on to study at Masters and at Doctorate level. They still relied on some financial support from their mothers.

Decisions about the Family Home

Studies in Ireland (Hogan *et al.*, 2002; Coulter, 2008; Mahon and Moore, 2011) show that, in the vast majority of cases, mothers remain in the family home with their children following separation. In this study nine of the fourteen women remained in the family homes following separation. For Geraldine and Mary part of their separation agreements was that their homes would have to be sold and the money divided once the youngest child reaches eighteen or twenty-three years of age (if in education).Of the five who moved house, two were in a position to buy their own houses (but will have mortgages to pay until they are seventy) and the remaining three are in temporary private-rented accommodation.

> BREDA: The family home is still waiting to be sold. As part of the divorce agreement, I am to get 55% and he is to get 45% but that is still waiting to be sold. One of the other things that happened at the time was I had the opportunity to live in a relative's house. Because I think if I hadn't had any place to go, I probably wouldn't have gone.
> L: He wasn't going and you had a place to go?
> BREDA: Yes. I had a place to go which is kind of a temporary arrangement still. So it's very insecure.

That Breda said she might not have left home if it she had not got a house to go to is a noteworthy comment as it raises questions about whether women leave their marriages because they can or whether other women stay because they have no money and no place to go.

One feature of separating after so many years of marriage was that the couples either had no mortgages or had very small amounts outstanding on their homes. Women were, therefore, in a better financial position to pay their husbands for their shares of the houses or to pay for alternative housing. Four of the husbands remained in the family homes after their wives left. Two bought new houses, six were living with new partners in private-rented accommodation and two were living alone in privately rented apartments.

The desire to retain their homes for the sake of their children and for themselves was mentioned by several of the women. Smart (2007) talks about a home being far more than a house; it contains family history and possessions to which meanings and memories attach. For children, their home represents security and continuity. The extent to which children's lives change on a daily basis has been found to be a key factor in how they adapt to separation (Hogan *et al.*, 2002). A change of house might also mean a change of school and the loss of friends. Most of the mothers were anxious to avoid that level of change all at once, both for their own sakes and for their children's sake.

> L: How important is it to you to hold onto this family home?
> HELEN: Oh, I want this. It's quite big, it's a big house. Somebody said to me recently 'will you stay there?' I may not but at the moment it's the girls' home. Ok, my eldest girl is away. I don't know whether she'll come back or not. I have two other girls. Their friends are around and everything like that but I want it, yes, I want it.
> L: Did he give back the key?
> HELEN: No ... At the mediation, he was having a strop about not giving back the key and, the only thing your man said in my defence was 'people should give back the key, if they're not planning to live there'.

> FRANCES: Our house had been up for sale about a year at this stage and it had sold five times. I just could not sign on the dotted line. I couldn't let go of my family home, my memories, my children's. Could not do it. Didn't want to know. And I tried everything to hold onto my home.

Frances is expressing the deep sense of loss she felt at having to sell her home. She clearly ascribed important meaning to the house in which she and her husband had raised their children together. She described the night she sold her house and signed her separation agreement as the 'darkest night of her life'. She officially lost her husband and her home on the same day.

Smart (2007) also talks about how the meaning and feelings associated with a family home may change following an event like a separation. Following divorce, the sorting out is forced rather than undertaken voluntarily. Feelings of hurt, pain and regret are revived. 'This forced sharing out of possessions is in effect a dismantling of what was planned to be a joint future' (Smart, 2007:169). Some of the women wanted to hold onto their homes at all costs, others no longer felt the same about their houses and wondered if they might be better to sell.

> DEIRDRE: In the last couple of years I would have felt that I would like to move out of here and make a fresh start in a new house but the way things went, it's just not the time.

According to Smart (2007), the sorting out of things becomes a metaphor for the sorting out of relations and memories. Clearing out the clutter of previous relationships often comes to symbolise a way of moving on and making a new beginning.

> L: What about the fact that it's full of memories of him? Does that bother you?
> HELEN: No because he wouldn't have had much to do with deciding things. It would have been me that would have done it.
> L: Have you taken down his photographs off the wall?
> HELEN: Yes. I didn't do it all at once, for the girls' sake. Family pictures, family occasions have gradually come down. I wanted to change my bedroom instantly. I painted it and re-arranged the furniture.

Because Helen's husband had been absent from home so often, he had not left his mark on it to any great extent. She felt it was hers. Courts may or may not take the same view about the meaning of family homes. According to Mahon and Moore (2011), in family law cases, family homes are treated as assets which women are granted in lieu of maintenance. The presumption is that the women can sell their homes and liquidate their asset. Some of the women did not see selling their home as an option. They saw it as being too important to their sense of security and as constituting too much loss at one time.

The other issue that arose in relation to houses was the issue of maintenance. Some women were initially at a loss when they could no longer rely on their husbands to fix things around the house. Catherine described how if a picture fell off the wall, she was convinced that this meant that the roof was about to fall in.

> CATHERINE: If a picture fell off the wall I was crying, whinging that the roof was going to fall in. Everything was exaggerated.

Jane said that she had lost interest in the house because she could no longer afford to keep it to the standard she wanted.

> JANE: I feel my house needs to be painted, the blinds are torn and he knows I have pride in this house. To me now I haven't, it's clean but I have no interest in the house anymore, because it's not to the standard, you know.

Geraldine and Helen also described some of the costs involved in maintaining an older house

> GERALDINE: I have this forty year old house that needs a lot of work done to it. I'm advised not to put money into it 'cos it won't hold its value. But still I'm going to live in a comfortable house for the next seven years ... I got an electrician ... and it cost 170 euros. That's not bad for what he did but it's still a 170 euros that I haven't otherwise got. Like I'm really tight for funds.

> HELEN: Maintenance is a big problem. I had a huge problem with shores and things while one of my daughters was sick. It cost me over two and a half thousand to get it sorted. There was a rat and everything involved and that was horrendous and with a sick child ... It's just everything you have to do. I know there's a thing with the sink now and it's going to go and I'm saying 'oh, no'. It's just everything ... My brother-in-law, who is his brother, is the only one of his family to have done anything to help. He's fantastic ... I was watching a programme about a DIY shop and ... I said 'I'm going to do a course in September to learn basic things like how to put a thing on the wall'.

While initially the women worried about who they were going to get to fix things in the house and how they were going to pay for house repairs and maintenance, in time, they sourced people who could help and were pleased with their ability to manage things that they had never done before. Their confidence in their ability to manage on their own seemed to increase with time. It was part of them developing a new identity which did not depend on a husband to fix things.

Income

Table 2 shows that nine of the fourteen women are employed full-time, seven in professional capacities and two in secretarial positions. Two of the women are part-time shop assistants, another is a part-time care assistant, another is a part-time student (ex-business executive) and another is in receipt of Carer's Allowance. The numbers in employment (9 full-time and 2 part-time) are higher than the national figure for female employment which stood at 56.4% in 2011 (CSO, 2011). In his comparative study of separation across Europe in 2004, Uunk found that in Denmark, Finland and Portugal, two-thirds of the women worked in paid employment prior to divorce, whereas in Ireland, half of the women worked before separation. The figures for this study are closer to the other European countries than to the Irish figures and are, again, indicative of the middle class backgrounds of the participants.

In relation to finalised legal settlements about maintenance, six (Anne, Breda, Catherine, Frances, Helen, Irene) of the fourteen women stated that they were getting nothing (neither for themselves nor their children) from their husbands. For some, who were working full-time and had good salaries and for Mary who got a lump sum settlement, the lack of maintenance was not a major problem. A further six women were getting some help towards costs for children who were still in third-level education. Some of these couples had worked out financial arrangements in mediated agreements which were working very well.

> DEIRDRE: He still gives me some maintenance.
> L: Is that for the children because they are still in College?
> DEIRDRE: Yes ... well we work the college part of it out separately. When fees arise, we pay half. We kept an account to do with all that and we each put in the

amount that's needed. So we set all that up properly ... He's very willing to help financially.

L: What are the conditions of your separation agreement?
SARAH: The conditions are; no maintenance for me, maintenance for the two children until they were finished college
L: And they were with you?
SARAH: No, they were shared between us. One was finished, she had finished her college, and one was two years into it and the other one at Leaving Cert. So we were to divide their maintenance between us. When they lived with whatever parent, they were supported by that parent, but medical, glasses, college fees, they were all to be split, half and half.

But others stated that they were struggling financially and that financial arrangements were a continuing source of contention.

BREDA: We separated and divorced at the same time in 2007 and he has never paid a penny maintenance for me or for my daughter.
L: Even though she has special needs?
BREDA: It doesn't make a difference once she is over eighteen. The roof over my head is not secure. I have no income into the future apart from Social Welfare. I am worried about what will happen to my daughter if I get sick ...

GERALDINE: When we had our judicial separation, the judge decided he should pay me 500 euros a month to be divided equally between the three children. Now 3 does not go into 500, that's all I get ... I pay all the bills on 500 a month. And once my eldest reaches 23, it will be one-third less and I don't know how I'm going to manage. I'm going to have to keep working. I'm not on the bread line. I have a permanent and pensionable job. It looks as if I'm going to be working full-time unless I win the lotto or something!

Eileen, Jane and Helen had very little money to live on while they were waiting for matters to be sorted out in court. All three had stayed at home to raise their children and were only able to find part-time, low-paid jobs, despite Eileen and Jane having third level qualifications.

JANE: Now, this present moment my husband gives me one hundred euros a week. One hundred euros a week. I work part-time, 20 hours a week. That's what I survive on. He's starving me of money, and if I had my way, I'd say, 'keep the 100 euros, I don't want anything off you', but I need the 100 euros.

The only maintenance Eileen got was that her rent was paid by her husband:

> EILEEN: I needed money to move out ... I went to see a solicitor and I came back and I told him. I couldn't believe how I had suddenly gone from being this invisible person to having a voice ... I know it's a bad time to be separating. I am basically on my own now ... I suppose one of the things I do worry about is whether he will continue to pay the rent each month.

Moore (2010) found that in some cases men connect maintenance payments to access/contact with children. This was Helen's experience.

> HELEN: He has used money at various times to try and get back at me ... When our eldest girl refused to speak with him, he cut maintenance off totally. He told me when I made her start speaking to him again he would start paying maintenance again. I had to go to Court over that ... The eldest girl was twenty three in November. He stopped her portion in September with no word to me and when the solicitor wrote to him he said 'she's finished her degree'. It didn't matter that she's not working or anything like that. I still support her, not totally, but she hasn't got a job in her field yet but she has a minimum pay job and she's struggling and I'm still supporting her ... I'm just about getting by.

Having spent fifteen years at home caring for her children, Helen felt she was lacking in the confidence and skills to get employment.

> HELEN: You're back down at the bottom of the ladder again. There wasn't even a computer in the office when I left ... Confidence was a big thing. I went back and I did the ECDL course in the summer before I started back and that gave me a bit ... He always made out that I was stupid and that he was the clever one, even though I did far better than him in school ...

The impact of the economic recession in Ireland can be seen in some of these quotations. Adult children, many of whom are graduates, are struggling to get well-paid jobs in their fields and are spending periods abroad, interspersed with periods living back at home with their mothers. Women in insecure employment are also struggling to find positions that match their qualifications and enable them to make ends meet.

While most of the women had experience of managing their own money, Geraldine and Jane described how little experience they had of managing complex financial matters. During their marriages, their husbands had taken responsibility for most things concerned with finances.

> GERALDINE: I found it very, very scary the whole thing about managing parenting, managing a home and finances. Like before we split up, every bill that came into the house I passed across the table. I never had to worry about that, ever. I had money, my money, for groceries and stuff like that but he paid all the bills. Now I have all that responsibility.

> JANE: I was at home ... You know what I mean, I left everything to him, financially. I didn't own my own bank account, do you know what I'm saying, I was happy ... All that shock ... I had to go to the bank, my god, I had to do this ... but I don't owe anyone a penny. All I owe is the solicitor's money, but I don't know where I'm going to get it. I do without too. You surprise yourself.

Helen had never bought a car when her husband lived with her. It was always her husband who sourced cars and negotiated deals. As with learning how to maintain her house, she has also learned how to buy a car.

> L: And you were saying, you were able to change the car yourself. You did the deal with the garage?
> HELEN: Yes, obviously I know the guy but, still, it was my first time ever to do that. It was nerve racking. My cousin's husband is in a garage and I rang him and he looked out and looked out and he got me the best deal, a really, really good deal.

The maintenance arrangements described in this study are similar to those found in a study of eighty-seven family law cases which was carried out by Mahon and Moore (2011). Mahon and Moore found that it was very rare for maintenance to be awarded to separating wives. Maintenance was only awarded to wives in 2 out of the 87 cases they observed. Such evidence contradicts popular opinion to the contrary. There is an assumption that maintenance payments for wives are common when, in fact, they are very rare. Mahon and Moore (2011) found that the women tended to get the family home in lieu of maintenance. They stated that '[t]here is little compensatory or rehabilitative support for ex-wives' (p. 81). Compensatory support refers to a model whereby women are compensated for loss of earnings due to household and childcare responsibilities during the marriage.

From the figures given, it would appear that this model is being eroded (Mahon and Moore, 2011). Rehabilitative support refers to a model whereby maintenance is given for a few years in order to help a woman find her feet financially, but after that period the expectation is that she should be able to support herself. They concluded that 'maintenance payments to wives are very rare and a degree of self-sufficiency, later if not sooner, is expected of them, even if they have been full-time carers of their children' (Mahon and Moore, 2011: 54). The notion that women are 'alimony drones' (Smart, 1999) and that divorce gives them a 'meal ticket for life' (Martin, 2002) are not borne out.

There is very little evidence in this study of either compensatory or rehabilitative payments being made to women in recognition of the time they spent caring for their children or in recognition of the difficulties they might face in re-entering the jobs market. Sheehan and Fehlberg (2000) also drew attention to problems with the 'equal treatment' approach taken in family law cases in Australia. They point out that the two usual pathways out of poverty, working and re-partnering, may not be options for women due to caring responsibilities for family members. Women who separate in midlife may not have caring responsibilities for children but they may find it difficult to find work and are also 'more likely to have difficulty finding new mates to share their economic burdens with' than younger women (Hilton and Anderson, 2009:312).

The difficulty with arguments favouring an 'equal treatment' approach is that women with children have not had equal access to employment because of the lack of childcare in Ireland and because of the traditional construction of gender roles which dictated that the mother was the parent who would stay at home in order to care for the children. Women who are in midlife may struggle to become self-sufficient in the current economic climate and the expectation that they would do so may be founded on unfair assumptions about gender equality, which failed to recognise the full context of their lives up to that point.

In terms of pension provision, six women (Anne, Deirdre, Sarah, Kay, Geraldine and Irene) stated that they will have full pensions on retirement. Kay will have a full pension, but her husband will be entitled to a portion of it.

KAY: He had sold pensions himself, and refused to buy one, and now suddenly 'I don't have a very big pension 'cos we couldn't afford it,' so he came after my pension, which I have never forgiven him for. I've gotten over it but I just think it was such a mean thing to do ...

L: So he got a lean on your pension

KAY: He has 26%/27% of my pension and of the gratuity, and my pension when I'm dead ... the death benefits, even though we are divorced. He insisted on that last bit which I felt was really ... Because I made the point that if I remarry I would like my then spouse to get that and he refused, and that wasn't him. He was a generous person, he just got into this victim mode ...

Two of the women (Catherine and Frances) entered the workforce later and will have small pensions. The presumption in Catherine's case was that she would share her husband's occupational pension.

CATHERINE: I have no pension. I'm in my job thirteen years. My pension wouldn't be a great pension but we would have largely talked about my pension being on top of his pension. He is now retiring.

Four (Breda, Helen, Jane and Nora) have no pension provisions and Mary hopes to live off the lump sum settlement from her divorce. This pattern of pension provision is similar to that found in a study by Hilton and Anderson (2009) in Nevada. They found that women in midlife had fewer pension entitlements (due to interrupted or part-time work histories) and less time to save for retirement. Breda, Helen, Jane and Nora all had interrupted or part-time work histories. Nora also had a period of sick leave which affected her Social Welfare contributions. Hilton and Anderson (2009) also found that women who separated in midlife were more likely to be living alone which is more costly than if living costs can be shared. A number of the women are expecting to live alone once their adult children leave home.

Several of the women commented that 'this should have been their time' (Nora). With the mortgage paid and the children reared, there should have been money for holidays together and to be able to look forward to retirement.

DEIRDRE: Financially, I am now watching my friends with all their mortgages paid off and having two and three holidays a year. They don't have to worry about the recession because it doesn't really affect them ... Had everything worked out nicely, I have my thirty five years done and I could retire now this summer, but on a lower pension. It would have been lovely and that's one of the things that makes me kind of sad and if I had a husband who was retired and had our mortgage paid and life would be so much different.

Instead the women needed to continue to work full-time for as long as possible and were facing into retirement alone and, in some cases, with a mortgage and inadequate pension cover.

Discussion: Public Endings and Division of Assets

The underlying concept is transition with the focus on loss but also on new beginnings. Transition suggests that separation is not just the end of a marriage but is also the beginning of a new life for both spouses. Legal proceedings involve a public ending of a marriage and division of assets with a view to future needs. As such, court attendance signifies an ending but also a new beginning. It marks a clear point in the process of transition to a different future.

Separation entails coming to terms with a series of losses and involves an emotional process which is similar in many respects to coming to terms with bereavement (Ahrons, 2005; Fisher and Alberti, 2006; O'Hara, 2011). For the women in this study marriage largely began in a church with family and friends celebrating together. Marriage entailed a public commitment and a promise for the future. Ceremonies expressing commitment generally take place in public and are relational events set within networks of friends and family (Smart, 2007). Legal separation and divorce take place in private in a court room. There are no communal rituals to support the people who are separating. Legal proceedings signify the official breakdown of a relationship. They necessitate talking about private troubles to strangers and the attendant upset that this may entail. They make separation a reality. There is no place within the legal process to deal with the emotional aspects of separating. Mediation is recommended as a support to the legal process but it too focuses solely on practical issues. Negotiating agreements assume that the parties are in a fit state emotionally to be able to communicate with each other and to plan together for the future. This was not the case in eleven of the fourteen cases presented in this dissertation. The emotional upset got in the way.

Access to children, maintenance of dependents and division of the family home are the issues which are generally dealt with in a legal context (Coulter, 2008; Moore and Mahon, 2011). As Smart (2007) pointed out, the dividing out of 'things' becomes a metaphor for the sorting out of past relations, meaning is ascribed to money and to family homes and these are linked to relationship issues during marriage. In this study, access to children was not decided by the courts as all of the children were teenagers and young adults. A consistent finding that emerged from the literature was that women are less well-off financially following separation (Amato, 2000; Weston and Smyth, 2000; Uunk, 2004). A finding that is emerging from recent Irish studies on family law cases (Hogan *et al.*, 2002; Coulter, 2008; Mahon and Moore, 2011) is that women and children generally stay in the family home and that very little maintenance is paid to women. As shown, all of these findings are replicated to some extent in this study.

The women in this study are clearly less secure financially than if they had stayed married but the majority could not be described as being in poverty. These women are atypical of women in Ireland in that so many of them have professional qualifications and worked full-time during their marriages. The women who left full-time work to care for their children are in the most precarious financial position. They are struggling to find steady employment. They have expenses in maintaining family homes and in supporting young adults who are not yet fully financially independent. They are facing into retirement with no occupational pensions. For many of the women, decisions about accommodation and finance are still pending and are an on-going source of stress and uncertainty.

As well as signifying loss, legal proceedings can also signify closure and planning for a new beginning. The focus in no-fault divorce proceedings is on future needs rather than on past misdemeanours. As will be shown in the next section, while the women worried about their changing financial and housing situations, it was the loss of relationships, the shifts in identity, and the emotional aspects of separation that they found the most difficult.

CHAPTER 8

Relationships following Separation

This chapter will consider data about the women's relationships following separation. Women are often deeply embedded in their relationships with family and friends. The breakup of a relationship constitutes a major event in their lives and has consequences for their other relationships. This chapter will focus on exploring the fourth research question about how family practices and relationships are constituted after a marriage breaks down. It will consider the extent to which relationships remain connected or are fragmented or reconstituted differently following separation.

Contact with Ex-Husband

The language used in marriage ceremonies uses phrases like 'two becoming one'. The symbols used echo the same theme: individual candles are often used to light a single bigger candle. The question this chapter addresses is what happens when the flame goes out on the big new candle. Do people just revert to being the individual 'candles' they were before? Do they become new 'candles'? Do they retain any connections to the 'couple candle'? Carter and Mc Goldrick (2005) suggest that the emotional work of divorce entails the retrieval of self from the marriage and the construction by each partner of a different identity and different dreams for the future. They are talking about constructing different 'candles'.

One factor that affects the shape of a family following separation is the extent to which a couple who have been married in excess of twenty years relate to each other following separation. Nine (Anne, Breda, Eileen, Frances, Geraldine, Helen, Irene, Jane and Kay) out of the fourteen women have little or no contact with their husbands/ex-husbands. In the six cases of infidelity by the husband, there is almost (Catherine and Nora being the exceptions) no contact. Where couples separate following infidelity, Scuka (2015) states that their level of contact varies along a spectrum. At one extreme, there may be no contact. In the middle, there may be 'a kind of civil acceptance of the other person ... with occasional and polite, if not cordial contact' (p. 166). At the other end there may be an element of 'genuine healing and ... an ability to be in the presence of the other person without feelings of resentment (p. 166).

Fischer *et al.* (2005) surveyed 1,791 Dutch people about contact with their ex-spouses following divorce. They found that almost half the couples still had some contact with their ex-husband/wife ten years after the divorce. The figure for contact in this study is less than the half found in the Dutch study. This is how six of the women described their current lack of contact with their ex-spouses.

ANNE: I have no contact at the moment.

BREDA: ... We very rarely talk to each other ... I find it very difficult ...

EILEEN: At the moment, I really don't want to have anything to do with him ... At the moment, things are not great. I just can't do it.

GERALDINE: I don't talk to his father anyway ... Every time I made contact I always felt like I was the baddie at the end of the conversation ...

HELEN: I haven't actually spoken to him in three years. I saw him last year down in the courts and it was the first time I had seen him.

KAY: He finds it very stressful meeting me, so he won't meet me.

The following quotation illustrates how Irene described setting some ground rules about contact.

IRENE: You don't come near the house. If you pick the kids up you stay on the road, do not come to the door. I don't want any correspondence with you. If anything happens to any of the kids I will phone you or I'll text you or I'll email you. But unless it's something official I don't want anything to do with you. As far as I'm concerned, you have died ... I have bumped into him when I've been out on different nights ... and it's very much as if I was meeting a stranger.

In some of these cases, husbands having met new partners were cited as reasons for having very little contact.

FRANCES: I haven't spoken to him since this time last year. I felt it wasn't my place to ring him.
L: So you don't have text contact, email contact?
FRANCES: Nothing. I might as well not exist.
L: And that's his..?
FRANCES: That's his wish because he's with somebody new.

JANE: We don't even talk now and there's no relationship with his children. There's nothing. He's living with a girl, and this is his fourth woman since he's left me.

The women who initiated separation hoped that their relationships with their husbands would be amicable and that they would be able to continue to attend family events together following separation but it did not always work out that way.

EILEEN: But I was the one who said before 'this has to be amicable because of the children and we're going to have celebrations etc, etc.' ... I need to be strong to meet him.

SARAH: I thought we would become civil, that was what I would have hoped for, that we could have been civil. He is still the broken-hearted man, too raw, that's what the girls say, too raw. This is what he says. He plays the victim, big time, and that upset me at the beginning.

Having to make arrangements about access for younger children is usually the focus of contact between parents following separation (Silva and Smart, 1999; Mahon and Moore, 2011). Most of the women in this study had older teenagers or young adults at the time of their separations so the children could make their own arrangements to see their fathers. Fathers could contact their children directly on the children's mobile phones. They

could make arrangements to meet in neutral venues without the mothers
having to get involved.

> IRENE: Occasionally he met them but there was no real planning. Now I didn't say
> anything about it. They're adults. I was having to stand by.

Even for the women who had some contact with their ex-husbands, the
encounters were described as being upsetting.

> CATHERINE: I bumped into him in the supermarket on Sunday night. He is always
> so glad to see me. He said 'ah hiya' and it's all such a bloody waste.
> L: Are you glad to see him?
> S: I'm craving him. It's like as if I'm parched. I'm quite pathetic.

> DEIRDRE: Strangely enough, he has never been nicer to me than he is now. He
> shows such concern, such care, in the last two or three years. It just seems so strange
> ... Sometimes even, an odd time, the two of us might just go out for a meal together
> but I find it a bit of a strain. I still find myself irritated by him and I wouldn't be
> totally relaxed. But I don't mind doing it either.

> NORA: My problem is my daughter doesn't want to see him, so he can never come
> if she is here. But I haven't got a problem. No, I'll give him his due: he will come
> and do whatever. He's come. He's changed bulbs. He's gone up in the attic for me.

The passage of time was mentioned as a factor that affected how some of
the women felt about contact with their former spouses.

> L: How much contact do you have now?
> CATHERINE: That's shifted and changed over the year. In the beginning I couldn't
> see him at all. I just couldn't see him. I was too hurt and then, I don't know at what
> stage, I saw him every so often. We'd go for a walk or we'd go for a meal but it was
> aimless because it was just being cast adrift from this man I was married to. You know
> you can't talk about tomorrow.

The reality of the women's lives following separation was that most (9) of
them had no contact with their ex-husbands and it was easier for them,
for a variety of reasons, to live without contact. Yet they felt blamed for
taking this position and that somehow they were not 'doing separation' in
the correct fashion if they were not communicating with their children's

fathers. They felt that there were cultural norms developing about the 'correct' way to do separation.

> HELEN: I'm not doing it right. I'm doing it completely against the book. I had a bit of a barney with someone recently, she turned and threw back at me 'well, you're doing it all wrong'.

Smart (1999) talks about how 'the rise of mediation and the demise of the emphasis on fault show a trend towards governing divorce in a manner that minimises conflict for the sake of the children' (Smart, 1999: 12). The Irish Family Mediation Service (<www.legalaidboard.ie>) also 'encourages the separating couple to co-operate with each other in working out mutually acceptable arrangements'. The message coming through is that couples should be able to communicate with each other following separation. As Helen put it;

> HELEN: If we were able to communicate, our marriages would not have broken down. The assumption always is (and if you hear people on the radio, the likes of Pat Kenny, I could throw a brick at the radio) that parents should talk to each other and work it out. Your marriage breaks up because you are not getting on so that doesn't work.

Moore (2010) reiterates the point that Helen is making. Moore found that patterns established during marriages carried over into post-separation practices and relationships. For the women in this study who had no contact with their ex-husbands, the sense of failure was increased by their inability to comply with the expectation of having a harmonious divorce. Not only had they failed in their marriages but now they were failing in their separations.

Post-Separation Parenting: Connectedness to Children

Almost all of the mothers in the sample continued to have close relationships with their children following separation. Some (Jane, Helen, Mary) would say that the relationships had become even closer in the absence of the fathers.

L: Has it brought you and the girls closer?
JANE: Oh my God! I went out with them there about three weeks ago ... The openness, even their friends say, 'Oh, my God, 'such a difference, look when he's not here'. My sisters say the same. Its only when he was gone, it made me see how uneasy he was.

HELEN: I find that we have become real close, the four of us ... We have got very close and we have spoken more.

MARY: All I can say is the day he left here the stress level in this house (even though it was stressful separating) went down. My daughter and I have a much calmer feeling and everything in the house from the day he left ... I realised I was starting to fight with her as well, I stopped myself ... But he was still fighting with her. This was when he was still here. So that really had helped me because by the time he left, she and I were communicating so much ... But we have a pretty good relationship.

The mothers talked about there being less tension in their houses and that they no longer had to mediate between their husbands and their children. Most of the children stayed in the family home with their mothers following separation. Those who were at an age to have left home, continued to return to be with their mothers for holidays and to celebrate family events. Being a mother continued to be a central aspect of the women's identities.

Eileen and Sarah, who left their homes, had the greatest difficulty in their subsequent relationships with their children. While the mothers were upset by their children's anger at them for leaving, they also understood it and felt that their children just needed time to come to terms with their reasons for leaving.

L: Were you taken aback then by your children's negative reaction?
EILEEN: Yes, when I moved I thought they would be coming and staying with me for holidays. I didn't see the implications of 'I don't want to talk to you'. They were talking to their Dad. He was always the victim so they heard what he was feeling. He was the victim, he had been damaged and they were supporting him. I found that very hard.

Sarah talked about how guilty she felt about putting her children in the position where they had to figure out how much time to spend with each parent and which house was their home.

SARAH: I'm very concerned about the damage it did to the kids, and I'm feeling more sorry about that now and I'm feeling guilty. I'm sorry that I had to put them through that. I don't like the fact that they now have to choose, when they come back from holidays, which house do they go to first, and Easter, where do they go. I don't like the fact that they have to choose that.

In the other two cases (Anne and Breda) where the women left home, the daughters went with the mothers and the sons (who were older) stayed with the fathers.

In four of the fourteen families, some or all of the children have refused to have anything to do with their fathers. These would be termed 'excluded fathers' (Moore, 2010: 264), except that in these cases it was not the mother who had excluded the father, it was the children. Moore's thesis that contact following separation depends on the quality of the relationships between fathers and their children before separation is also not entirely borne out. As the following quotations will demonstrate, some of the children who refused contact with their fathers were children whose relationships with their fathers had been extremely close prior to separation.

GERALDINE: My oldest son who was the best friend of his father, adored his father, can't stand him now. He doesn't want to have anything to do with him. He is just excluded. He can have the hump all he likes about being excluded but that's the way it is. The other two are different. They still see him and they still have regular contact.

Again in Helen's case the youngest of the three girls was the only one who would see her father.

HELEN: She sees him for an hour every three weeks or once a month, that's all. She said she sees him because she feels sorry for him because nobody else will see him.

In other cases (Frances, Irene and Kay) it is not that the children have refused contact but that their fathers have been very poor at continuing to make arrangements to meet them and the mothers are no longer prepared to do the work of mediating between their children and their fathers. Moore (2010) refers to 'contact sliding into absence' (p. 288).

FRANCES: Sean is not the type that would ring them very often. He might ring them once every three months. The last time he was down was this time last year and like he has a grandson a year old ... He was great with the children. They were a huge part of his life but once that kind of time came when they were at that age, he just didn't want that any more. He just felt 'now they're happy' and he wanted a new habitat ... He wanted to get away from any responsibility ... I feel bad that my children are not included in his life. I feel bad that my children are not really in touch with him. That's so awful to think that you brought them up in such a way and how lonely that must feel for them and such a loss. And if you were to meet anyone again, it could never be the same.

IRENE: He said to the kids that our relationship had totally broken down and he just wanted a different life. Now that they were all grown up, he felt confident that they'd make their own way in life.

In some cases the children are happy to meet their father but do not want to meet his new partner.

IRENE: The kids said 'no. I'm not going to meet you over there. I don't want to go there anymore' because he never was true to his word. She would always turn up at some stage of the evening. So they were uncomfortable with it, so that has stopped.

GERALDINE: There was a row about meeting up. When the two lads said to him 'sorry, don't want to meet her' ... I just let the lads tell me in their own way and they didn't want to tell me too much ... Then I said 'I don't want to hear this. This is not my business'. That's what's going on. That sort of tension is always going to be there ... They have to live with this for the rest of their lives. They are going to have to balance this always ... He is insisting that they meet her ... I can see that they are getting more hurt as the time goes on ...

Several of the women talked about how difficult it had become to talk openly to their children about things in relation to their fathers or their new living arrangements. They described how they wanted to have open and honest relationships with their children but that there were now a range of topics, relating to their fathers' current lifestyles, which they could not discuss. Catherine described how she wanted to help her daughter with her new house but that she was hesitant to visit because her husband might be there helping with the renovations. She also described her upset that they could not share their joy at the birth of their first grandson.

CATHERINE: My son's girlfriend had a baby and I found that certainly hurtful not to be able to share it ... That night I was kind of waiting ... my son's baby was coming home. I got a text and it was a picture of my granddaughter holding my brand new grandson. Obviously Dennis was there. It wasn't in the hospital. They had called round to him. I was totally devastated. I was totally, totally upset ... I was just hurt. I said 'how could they do all that and leave me out?' ... When my son rang he said 'look Mam, Dad rang just as we were coming home and said would we swing by'. He said 'Mam, I always wanted you to be the first to see the baby.' I said 'no, that's fine' but I was so hurt ...

The mothers understood that their children were in a very difficult situation, trying to be loyal to both parents and being unsure of what information they should pass on and what information they should keep to themselves.

IRENE: He had already met the kids and asked them to promise not to tell me that this one was pregnant. They didn't tell me which I must say I was hurt at ... I was a bit taken aback because I didn't think they kept any secrets from me. I was very open with them ... but then they are stuck between the two and where do their loyalties lie?

KAY: Then when he started dating his new partner, who is a colleague who works with him, he told her (his daughter) and she didn't know whether to tell me or not, and then trying to figure it out, she stopped talking to me, because she didn't know ...

Due to most of the children being teenagers or young adults when their parents separated, they could make their own decisions about how much contact they wanted to maintain with their parents. Many of the children had left home and had very different levels of contact with parents than if they were younger. A majority of the mothers in the study felt, after some initial difficulties and despite the complexities of their new living situations, that they had maintained close relationships with their children following separation.

The situation with the fathers was somewhat different. Eight out of a total of thirty-five children opted to have nothing to do with their fathers. In situations where the fathers had new partners or had moved away, the children had only sporadic contact. Only one couple (Mary), who had the youngest child in the study, came close to having an egalitarian post-separation parenting style.

Recent Irish research (Hogan *et al.*, 2002; Timonen *et al.*, 2009; Mahon and Moore, 2011) has tended to focus on the needs of younger children whose parents separate than on the age group of young adults described by the mothers in this study. How children reacted to separations clearly had an impact on how the women coped. The mothers told stories of children failing exams, dropping out of college, becoming anorexic and binge drinking. These things might have happened in any event but the mothers felt some of their children's difficulties were linked to their upset about their parents' separation.

> L: Were you connecting your daughter's sickness with your separation?
> HELEN: Oh it was, because of the fact that she wouldn't talk. She internalised it all and she even gets like that still because she doesn't talk to him ...

The children's upset clearly added to the women's upset. Much of their time and energy was spent trying to get help for their children and trying to shield them from further hurt. The women were at pains to point out that just because their children were older, it did not mean that parental separation did not hurt them. How adult children react to parental separation is a topic on which very little research has been conducted in Ireland. It is an area which was outside the scope of this study but, based on the difficulties described by the mothers, it is an area which needs further investigation so that support can be provided for young adults in this situation.

Renegotiating Family Events

Much of family life, memories of childhood and stories that form family history are structured around sharing and celebrating family events. 'Family rituals are central to the socialisation provided by the family, nurturing a sense of family identity and belonging and providing meaning to family interactions' (de Roiste, 2006:14). When a marriage breaks down, the structure of the family changes and arranging these events can become more complicated.

In only three (Catherine, Deirdre, Mary) of the fourteen families did both parents automatically celebrate events like Christmas, 21st birthdays, graduations, weddings or the birth of grandchildren together. In most cases, it was the fathers who were either not invited or who declined to attend.

> HELEN: He's been at nothing. We have a 'debs' coming up in a few weeks for the girl he sees but there is not a mention of him coming. We've had two graduations, an entrance scholarship to University and two debs without him. On a selfish point, I don't mind now because I don't have to look at him.

Jane has a daughter getting married.

> JANE: She's getting married this New Year's Eve. I love her to bits, but why this year? I have no money. I can't even think of it.
> L: How are you going to manage the wedding? Will her father be invited?
> JANE: No, no, no, and that's her choice. There's no relationship.

Even where fathers did attend, celebrations were tinged with sadness for 'what might have been'.

> CATHERINE: I just dreaded the wedding but it was a wonderful day. I came back here with my brother and his wife and Dennis came back here just to collect the keys of his car. When he left my sister-in-law just broke down and sobbed and sobbed and sobbed and I sobbed as well. My brother said 'I can't help you, ladies.' Then later on, about four in the morning, my brother started crying because Dennis was like his brother.

> SARAH: Interestingly enough, graduations, we are there for them and for the youngest one's 21st. I'm very happy there. I don't mind meeting him. He is the one that has huge problem with it. And with the last graduation, he wouldn't tell her, he didn't tell her even up to the day that he was coming because I think he's not able to see me. He just isn't able.

Eileen, who had initiated separation, was invited back home for Christmas but found it extremely difficult walking away on her own afterwards and feels she will never go back again for Christmas. In the first few years after separating, Christmas seems to be a particularly stressful time of the year, as Eileen, Kay and Sarah explain:

EILEEN: My children wanted me to go back for Christmas ... The most difficult thing I had to do when I was finished talking to them was I walked out the door and down the drive on my own and got into my car. That was so awful because they were up there with their father and I was walking away on my own.

KAY: Christmas is very, very difficult, very difficult and the first Christmas awful, I ended up bawling crying at the table.
L: Did you invite him?
KAY: I didn't, I purposely, – and I even told him he wasn't welcome, because I think he was expecting to be invited, and I said no. Because I had this thing that there is no point pretending, if it's not there it's not there, and maybe that was wrong ...

L: How did you get through the first Christmas, were you on our own?
SARAH: The eldest was away, but I went to my sister for the dinner, stayed overnight with her, came back the next day, and it was hard but you just get the first one over you and that's it, you just ... you're in a bit of state of shock I think.

Breda feels that Christmas does not get easier, even after several years.

L: One of the things that families find difficult following separation are family events like Christmas.
BREDA: Oh God yes and do you know what? Those things don't get any easier. What I found was those things are even getting worse. When I was studying and doing a degree, I had a focus, I had a goal and Christmas kind of took a back seat. One of the Christmases I was really depressed and I took myself off to my sister in the States ... I find those days difficult. I miss him. I miss him acutely ...

Family events not only involve happy events but also events where families come together as a unit to support each other at times of sickness or death. Several of the women discussed what they felt their response would be if their ex-husband became ill and needed care in the future. Deirdre's husband has been diagnosed with a serious illness. This was her response:

DEIRDRE: My first reaction was 'thank God this happened after we separated and not before' because I could never have gone through with the separation ... Brendan came home and said 'Who's going to look after Dad?' I was very taken aback by this and I felt he was implying 'what are you going to do about that?' I just said that of course I wouldn't see him stuck but that there was no way that he would be coming back to live here. I said 'he's got three sisters and two brothers'.

Deirdre was identifying that her obligation to care for her ex-husband had shifted since their separation and that the responsibility now shifted back to his family of origin. This is one of the freedoms that Bateson (2000) identifies which can result from a major change in a life trajectory. According to Bateson (2000: 53/54), '[e]very shift in the shape of lives proposes new understandings of freedom and shifts in the intersecting geometries of obligation and dependency'. Separated spouses are freed from the obligation to care for each other and for each other's families. In this context, Deirdre also stated that she often thought about how she felt she would behave at his funeral.

> DEIRDRE: Sometimes I imagine at his funeral (I know I shouldn't) which seat will I be in? Those things all go through your head.
> L: Do you imagine yourself at the top of the church as the chief mourner or hiding discreetly at the back of the church?
> DEIRDRE: At the back of the church is where I would like to be but I feel it would be such a difficult time for Brendan and Jenny that my place would be with them and that would put me at the top of the church. It's just one more of those rounds.

> L: Do you ever think 'if he got sick, would I go back and take care of him?'
> EILEEN: I have thought about it and, quite honestly, yes, if he was very ill, I would go back because I know he has nobody else. (Dare I say it?)
> L: If he died, where would you stand in the Church? Would you stand up at the top as the chief mourner with the children?
> EILEEN: I don't know, that would be up to the children but I would be there because that was a very important twenty eight years of my life.

Other women also said they had given consideration to how they would behave at their mother-in-laws' funerals.

> L: This might sound like a mad question, do you ever visualise his funeral and where you would stand in the church?
> JANE: No, but I visualise his mother's, it's in my head the whole time.
> L: And where are you going to be? How are you going to react?
> JANE: I'm not going to be there. I'm not going to be there, and I've asked my girls 'if Nanny dies, that's your choice lads. You're adults, that's your choice.

Jane was stating that she no longer belonged to her husband's family. She was re-configuring her family to just include her children and her own family of origin. She was drawing new boundaries around who was in her family and who was no longer in her family.

That only three of fourteen families shared celebrations together makes sense in the context of relations having broken down to the extent that they have in the families in this study. However, it does not comply with the ideal of 'harmonious' divorce espoused in current discourse. If conflict is seen as the aspect that causes the most harm in the separation process (Smart, 1999), then the ideal alternative being presented is that people should separate without conflict and should reconstitute their relationships in a harmonious manner.

Establishing harmonious relationships with ex-spouses does not seem to be happening for the vast majority of women in this study. It may be significant that Moore (2010) found that the couples she described as 'egalitarians' following separation tended to be in the younger age group. There may be a generational factor at play here. As Bateson (1989) says '[e]vents look different from the vantage point of different dates of birth' (p. 66). Fischer *et al.* (2005) found that people with liberal attitudes towards divorce were more likely to maintain contact with their ex-spouses and to believe that they could be friends following divorce than those with conservative views on separation. Embeddedness in traditional beliefs about lifelong marriage by the women in this study, along with the level of hurt experienced, may be impacting on how relationships are constructed following separation.

Initiators had hoped that relationships could be amicable. They referred to non-initiators who were not prepared to be amicable as 'playing the victim'. It is impossible to predict if this pattern will continue into the future. Fischer *et al.* (2005) found in the Netherlands that antagonism faded over time and that contact depended on the relationships that had existed during marriage, the presence or absence of a new partner and the presence or absence of joint children. Fischer *et al.* (2005) also found that both friendly and antagonistic contact lessened with the passage of time. For the women in this study, it is impossible to predict whether relationships will become even more distant over time or whether time will heal some of the pain, and family members will be able to attend family events together. Some of the women expressed a wish that relationships with former spouses and children might become easier in time.

> EILEEN: At the moment I am taking a break I have to strengthen myself. I do see that I will be going to these things but I need to be in a better place. I need to be able to talk to him. I don't want this to be awkward for my children. I want us to be friends but I am not in that place yet. I can't do that.

> GERALDINE: I wish they (her son and his father) could get back together because it's hard for both of them. Maybe it will happen, I hope it does for both their sakes but right now it's not.

> IRENE: But I don't think, when you have kids, that you can ever be divorced from that person really. They'll always be a part of your life. Maybe there will come a time when I'll be happy to meet him but at the moment I have to keep it a very business-like arrangement. And that's the way I want it to be. I hate the thought of the kids having extra relatives in their lives that are not part of our family but, you know, with the way life has moved on, I hope I'm not stuck back in the 50s.

Others felt that 'a line had been crossed' and the trust that had been betrayed would take a huge effort to rebuild. Many of the women felt that their husbands had become strangers to them and that they no longer recognised them as the men they had married. They could not envisage that the work required to rebuild trust would be undertaken.

Connectedness with Kin: Fear of Stigma

The women's families of origin were a major source of support for twelve of the fourteen women. The Timonen *et al.* (2009) study described grandparents in particular as 'the lynchpin' (p. xiv) of a support system that helped their children and their grandchildren to cope following separation. This source of support was not available to many of the women who separated in midlife as their parents had already died or were very elderly. Some of the women said they were glad their parents had not lived to see them separate as it would have upset them so much. They drew strength from their memories of their deceased parents. Others described how their parents were upset and possibly ashamed but not one parent turned against their child due to their becoming separated.

> L: What was their reaction, were they ashamed?
> JANE: No, not ashamed ... They were shocked, they felt rejected as much as I did. He was their son, they loved him ... My mother is so angry ...

> DEIRDRE: My mother was very slow to tell her sisters and her family. At some level she was probably ashamed or whatever. When things were bad in my marriage and I went through the separation I went over to her every Saturday evening for years and years and years. It was a life line. She'd say 'sit down there now and we'll have a cup of tea'. She was a very wise and very talented woman. I was trying to spare her from too much worry about me but I was able to tell her. Her death has affected me hugely.

> L: Do you think that they were very embarrassed in their community?
> KAY: I think they found it hard to tell people, yea ... They're very good in their own way, and their way is to organise family to come up and see me. They wouldn't talk about it ... I know I was down at some family celebration shortly afterwards, and literally if I was in the kitchen, it was if I was contagious. Nobody wanted to stay to be drawn into conversation. They all disappeared.
> L: So nobody knew what to say
> KAY: Nobody knew what to say. I can understand.
> L: Did you have any sense of personal failure to be in that situation?
> KAY: Tremendous! Tremendous. Yea, it was awful at the time.

Deirdre and Kay had originally come from rural areas and had moved away but their parents still lived in the same places. Geraldine's parents lived in an urban area but the reaction was similar.

> GERALDINE: They were devastated. My parents couldn't believe it. You see, I hid everything. I didn't say anything to anybody. They called it 'my situation'. They had very staunch Catholic views right up to a couple of years ago.
> L: Did they support you emotionally during and after the separation?
> GERALDINE: Depends what you mean by that. They weren't really able to support me in the sense that they were absolutely shocked and hurt and upset. It really did not fit into their norms and values but they didn't disown me. They were supportive but they were ashamed, even though they wouldn't like to say that ...

The reactions of parents described above as being 'devastated' and finding it 'hard to tell' reflects an older generation's attitudes to separation. While the parents did not blame their children, the women felt that they were embarrassed by their separating and that their parents still acted as if there was a stigma attached to separating. Some of the women said they worried that the stigma assumed by an older generation still existed and would attach to their children.

Sisters, rather than parents, emerged as the greatest source of support for most of the women. Many of them had confided in their sisters about how unhappy they were in their marriages before there was even a question of them separating. A recurring theme in the transcripts is that they had told almost nobody about how deeply unhappy they were in their marriages so their separations came as a shock to some family members and friends.

> ANNE: So when I moved out, we were in the hotel and I had brilliant support from my sisters. I think she [one sister in particular] really felt 'she's out now and I'm not letting her go back' ... I just had literally what we had in the suitcase ... My sister set me up with sheets and towels and delph and all of that and they were absolutely there for me.
> At the time I moved out I didn't actually get in touch with the people in Al Anon at that particular time because I was too broken. I just needed my family and my close friends.

> DEIRDRE: The only ones that really knew that I was in difficulties were my sisters, basically that was it. When we made the decision to separate and maybe even before that I would have had one or two friends that I would have talked to a bit. But some of the things that happened, nobody knew about ... Through it all I was able to ring them (my sisters) at any time and it's still the same.

> IRENE: My sisters, in particular my sister who is single, have been my rock of strength. My daughter has said she is better than any husband. She has been my strength going back.

Kay described her sisters coming to her house every weekend and ringing her every night to make sure that she was okay. Mary, who had lived outside the country for several years, found it hugely supportive to be back close to her family when she was going through her separation.

L: You were back in your home town but that could bring a negative in being ashamed.
MARY: Not in my family. There may be some people in the extended family who are judgemental (there's no question about that) but they would never say it to my face. But not my immediate family, not my sisters, 100% they would be behind me. They would never think 'oh you must have done something', never. I feel that for people who don't have a supportive family, I don't know how they get through it. If I didn't have my family I wouldn't have been able to cope.

Brothers were also a great support to many of the women but in a more practical way.

GERALDINE: My brother came with me on the day of my separation hearing and sort of sat with me and chatted and just stayed with me on that day ... the same on the divorce day ... Like I don't see him from one end of the year to another but I ring him and say 'this is coming up. Are you available?' 'Oh yes, of course.' It's great support I have to say.

KAY: Brothers, no, far more practical, they'd come up and I've a brother coming up on Friday to cut all the hedges, and all this kind of thing, you know. My younger brother, who isn't married, he'd made a point ... He was up for every match, he'd take me to the match and say we'd go for dinner afterwards, practical stuff. It was lovely!

MARY: It was mainly with my sisters, not 'cos my brothers are horrible, but you don't really talk about all that stuff with your brothers.

Helen and Nora described their parents and some siblings as being helpful but only 'up to a point'. Either they did not really understand how separating felt because they had not been through it themselves or they did not understand because the women in the study did not want to burden them and did not tell them the full extent of their upset.

HELEN: They were good to me to a point. My mother ... would never really turn around and say 'how are you doing now?' My Dad is very hurt ... He won't talk, I mean, he wouldn't talk like that but he will try and do everything else. He will always praise me.
My sister here and my brother did give me support ... but they could only give it to a point because they didn't understand. One of my other sisters (I could kill her at times) but she'd be looking for the gossip end of it, do you know what I mean?

NORA: My Mam is very helpful. She's ringing up all the time to see if I'm okay and are the girls okay. She'll be sending me a few pounds when she has it, you know. I don't want to be taking money off her ... She'd be saying to me: 'I'm sure you miss him' and I'd say: 'Of course I do, mother.' But she doesn't understand.

Frances described a scenario in which her separation has never been discussed with her siblings.

L: How did your family, your brothers and sisters react?
FRANCES: No reaction. They never, ever spoke about it which I find incredible. I remember the night that I sold my house and separated at the same time. I remember texting my family at about two o'clock in the morning and saying 'this has been one of the darkest days in my life'. Never, not a word. I suppose they didn't know what to say.

Eileen has had very little contact with her brother because his wife so disapproved of her decision to leave.

EILEEN: I only have two siblings, one of their spouses has taken very much his side ... I went to a funeral of a relation and I met up with people and they hadn't told anyone, my brother hadn't told anyone ...

Many Irish people do not know what to say when somebody separates. There was no culture of divorce here so there are no established conventions for how to react. People's unease may be a symptom of how uncomfortable people still are about separation. This silence leaves women not knowing what people are thinking and saying about them. This may lead to some women feeling unsupported or, on the other hand, they may see silence on the topic as a sign that their privacy is being respected.

Relationships with their husbands' families were closely connected with relationships with ex-husbands. In some cases where there was continued contact with husbands, there was also contact with his family.

CATHERINE: His family are wonderful to me. I meet his sister once a fortnight for lunch. She goes into town and meets me. They would ring me regularly. They would be very much there for me ...

KAY: My in-laws have been very good now, I have to say, very kind, and they're very good to the kids. They will always include them in everything ...

In cases where there was no relationship with the husband or, more particularly, between children and their father, there was no relationship with his family.

> JANE: They distanced themselves, you know, and his mother actually, and I passed her last Tuesday night, I was going for a walk with my friend, she got out of a taxi and turned her whole body away from me.

Ireland is still a country in which family affiliation is very important. If relationships with in-laws were good before separation, to lose them can be yet another significant loss, both for the woman and for her children.

Relationships in Work

Only two of the women in the study were not in employment. While some found it difficult to cope with the pressures at work and needed to take some time off at the time of their separations (Anne and Kay), most turned up every day and adopted their 'coping masks'. Each of the women told their bosses at work about their separations. All of them received understanding and supportive responses. The women who were teachers were very aware that being separated would have been considered something to be ashamed of in their profession in the past.

> L: How did your colleagues in work react?
> DEIRDRE: In the job I'm in there would have been a time when that would have been a huge scandal, you probably wouldn't say it. Our staff is a big staff and there was only one other girl on staff separated already. People were sympathetic.

> ANNE: I had to ring my boss and tell him and he was very supportive and told me to look after myself and my daughter and take whatever time was needed. I did go back then to working after two weeks but I really wasn't ready. I wasn't able for it ... I was an emotional wreck at that stage. I was just crying my eyes out all day long.

The way most of the women handled the news of their separations in work was that they told their closest colleagues and asked them to tell the others, but also to say that they did not wish to discuss the details any further.

> KAY: I was delighted to go back to work. It was just like wrapping myself with a blanket ... I spoke to one of the others and I said 'would you mind spreading the word and I really don't want to talk about it'. And she said 'fine' and she did that, and everybody was very good ...

> GERALDINE: One of the best things I did in supporting myself was that I was able to say straight away when he did leave, I said it to my boss. I said it to the schools, the football team and I got it out there immediately. There was no pussy footing around. I didn't care. I wasn't going to pretend anything.

The women asked for privacy and their wishes seem to have been respected. There are no rituals that people from work can attend to express their regret and support at the time of separation. There are no Mass cards they can send because nobody is dead. Several of the women stated that their work colleagues had become some of their closest friends and were supportive both inside and outside of work. Work was a key aspect of the women's identity, as well as being a source of income. It was important that work continued to be a positive place in the women's lives.

Social Life

The women talked about how necessary it is for women to keep their own friends and their own interests during marriage and not to be totally subsumed in their husband's social network.

> CATHERINE: It was important for me to have had a life of my own because I had all that network and that level of independence I could fall back on. They were always there.
> L: So while you were very much part of a couple since you were fifteen, you also had this other life?
> CATHERINE: Yes, without a doubt, and I say to my daughter 'hold onto your pals and keep those interests up'.

All of the women had the experience that they lost some joint friends as a result of separation.

If the women lived in a small community, this made it difficult to socialise if they were not on speaking terms with their ex-husband

> CATHERINE: In terms of mutual friends, well that's quite fractured. One couple that we were quite close to, I see her quite a lot. I wouldn't be friends with him at all.
> L: Used you go out with them as a couple?
> CATHERINE: Yes and we used to have people in and that has stopped.

> KAY: Socially, I've found it very hard. He was involved in sport. I've lost all those friends, I know nobody. I keep saying that I used to get three hundred Christmas cards, and I don't get thirty now. I was just left. His job would be very sociable, and all our going out would have to do with that, and that's a big loss in my life, because I enjoyed the whole social life that went with it. It's all a closed door to me now I feel, because it's a very small community really.

Some of the women described having to build their social lives almost from scratch after they separated. Breda went back to college and made an entire new circle of friends.

> BREDA: It wasn't so much that I lost friends, as that I removed myself. I went to college and would have shifted to a different way of socialising, socialising over coffee, socialising over assignments ... different.

Geraldine, Helen and Kay have got involved in a support group for separated and bereaved people called Beginning Experience (BE) and have built a social life around that organisation.

> GERALDINE: Socially, the B.E. crowd and there's a whole bunch of us actually in work that have become friends and we're all separated or divorced. We didn't purposely come together but it's like we found a level or a common ground. So I have friends but that's only built up over the last number of years and it hasn't been there for the whole time.

> HELEN: Meeting up with the B.E on a social level, that is a lot easier. We do things like going to the theatre, the cinema, walking. Hill walking is great.

Kay talks about how her friends are almost entirely female now. Helen described how she has purposely tried to socialise not just with her female friends but also to maintain her friendship with their husbands.

> KAY: I have a very small circle now and it's almost entirely female and that's a big lack. I really miss maleness.

> HELEN: I tend to do family things and things with my friends. Sometimes just the girls go out because five was an uneven number. I have initiated it recently and said 'no, I want the lads to come out as well' and we've done it occasionally as well.

A common reaction to separation is that people isolate themselves. Catherine talked about not wanting people in her house since her separation because she felt exposed and had less energy.

> CATHERINE: I don't want people in my house. I feel so exposed. It'll be just neighbours and I don't know if they know or not and I don't care if they know but I don't want them here ... It all takes energy and I don't really have it.

Deirdre talked about only barely managing to keep going, much less having the energy to throw herself into a whole new range of activities that involved meeting a group of new people.

> DEIRDRE: I have to say, ever since I separated, if another person says to me 'why don't you take up painting and hill walking?' ... as if that would be the answer to everything. I just said 'I don't want to paint or I don't want to hill walk'. There is this perception out there that suddenly because you're separated, you should just dive into all these. This has been horrific for me. I have just about kept my head above water.

Another difficulty the women referred to was that their married friends were not available to socialise with at night time or to go away with on holidays because they were taken up with activities in their families. Sundays were mentioned as particularly long and lonely days.

> JANE: What will I do here all day? I cleaned the hot press, cleaned that press and cleaned the cooker. I washed my handbags. I was going all day ... and then all night on my own. I could have rang my friends but they were all out, and I feel Sunday is a family day.

Some of the women said they disliked socialising with couples but that Ireland is still a very couples-oriented society.

> NORA: I have plenty of women to go away with, but I feel I actually hate going places where it's all couples.

Women who are 'single again' have trouble socialising. They do not 'fit'. They tend to rely primarily on female friends and family members. Several of the women listed their sisters, in particular single sisters, as being the mainstay of their social lives.

> DEIRDRE: It's my biggest problem at the moment, not having friends in the same situation. All my friends, people I work with, friends that I've had from school, are all still in their marriages. I mean I go out with them still and I meet up with them but nobody else has time, that's one of the biggest problems. My sister, who is separated, we would have gone once or twice. But even just the other day I saw a lovely deal on the paper for two nights down the country but I was looking at it and said 'I've nobody to go with'. I find that very upsetting.

> MARY: The friends I've made around here, a lot of them are married and some of them have younger kids so they're not going to do stuff with me at the weekend. I know them ... like daytime I can find people to play a game of tennis or go for lunch or go for a cup of coffee but night time or weekend, much more difficult ... I have a divorced sister as you know and her children are adults, they're grown up, she and I have gone away.

> KAY: I have two unmarried sisters, so I have someone to go travelling with. I have companionship of an order that I enjoy. We have great fun together. We enjoy each other's company.

None of the women were in new relationships. Five (Breda, Catherine, Frances, Irene and Nora) stated that they still loved their husbands and were having a hard time letting that go.

> CATHERINE: I want a relationship with my husband, right or wrong. It's too hard for me to let it go yet.

> IRENE: I haven't directed any of my anger really towards him. And I don't know why that is really, because way down I have a major grá (love) there for him. I'm not a person who destroyed anything to do with him, photographs or anything like that. I mean I want to savour the good times that we had. And I mourn that time really ...

The women acknowledged that their emotions were ambiguous and contradictory. They loved their husbands but hated aspects of their behaviour. It was as if they still held onto a hope that the men would change and 'come to their senses' one day. It was as if their husbands had become strangers to them and they wished they would revert back to their former kind and caring selves. This made it very difficult for the women to 'move on'. Most of them were scared of depending totally on a man again and said that they would never re-marry but would like to be involved in a relationship.

> DEIRDRE: In the beginning I said never again, I couldn't imagine ... and as the years have gone by ... I'd love the company. I'd never marry somebody else. I'd never want somebody else to come live in my house but I wouldn't rule out a male in my life, as a companion and maybe for more as well.

> FRANCES: I don't know that I would trust myself or anyone else, 'cos I suppose I still love him. I couldn't see myself having any meaningful relationship with any other man, unless somebody walked into my life and I was totally bowled over ... I wouldn't say 'no' to the possibility of a relationship but I wouldn't do the marriage thing. I'd never put myself through that.

> GERALDINE: I'm not looking for another man. I don't have one ... I'm not of the mind set at my age to find another man, as in 'find another man to pay the bills'. I would love the companionship. I would love to experience the closeness of a strong relationship ... You have to marry the rich widower, to be honest, because marrying a divorced man, he's paying the alimony or the maintenance or whatever you want to call it. Plus you have the whole care of his children and he wants to spend time with his kids. There might be issues ...

The women were very conscious that their age was a barrier to their chances of meeting another man.

> GERALDINE: A man our age wouldn't be bothered looking at us. He'd be more interested in a women half our age.

> MARY: If you're over forty five, you're too old. I think it's because fifty plus year old men don't want a woman of that age. They want somebody who is in their thirties. So they (dating agencies) don't get enough demand for it so anybody over forty-five is basically screwed. There's no place to go out and meet men, other than maybe going into some seedy bar or something.

Fine Davis (2011) surveyed 1,404 people in Ireland and found that single women who were in their late thirties were having difficulty finding partners. Like the women in this study, they felt that Irish men wanted younger women. The situation in the United States seems to be somewhat different. Brown and I-Fen Lin (2012) from Bowling Green State University presented a paper in April 2012 on 'The Gray Revolution'. They concluded that the rate of divorce among people in the over fifty age range in the US has increased to such an extent that there should be lots of single-again older people available for dating. This situation does not appear to exist in Ireland as yet.

Discussion: Fragmentation and Connectedness in Relationships following Separation

The data in this study show that relationships between former spouses may be seriously fragmented as a result of separation in midlife. Very few couples managed to remain on friendly terms with each other. Relationships between fathers and some of the adult children were also seriously fragmented following separation because some children refused to have anything to do with their fathers. Some relationships with in-laws were lost. Some relationships with joint friends were also lost. Social lives were disrupted. Some of the women felt they had to start from scratch to build their social lives as a result of separating.

Kalmijn (2010), writing about the differences between countries in Europe in terms of support following divorce, found that while the barriers to divorce are stronger in countries where family is strong, the support offered to their own members in the event of divorce is also stronger. The data in this study support that conclusion. All of the women stayed connected to their families of origin. Almost all of the women continued to be closely connected to their children. Most of the women and children stayed in the same house. Sisters and friends emerged as the most important sources of support. The women mentioned how important it had been to have maintained their own friends and their own interests throughout their married lives. All of the women continued to work, as they had done before their separations.

The stage in the life-cycle most of the families are at involves children graduating from school, from college, getting married and the parents becoming grandparents. This stage of the life-cycle may also involve grandparents becoming more dependent and dying. Family life goes on with everyday communication, occasional attendance at family events and obligations to provide care to dependent members, but former spouses may no longer be considered to belong to the family. This study has shown that different families adopt practices and organise family events in a variety of ways following separation.

CHAPTER 9

Identity and Resilience Post-Separation

The construction of individual identity develops through relationships with others. When a relationship breaks down, particularly a marital relationship, a major shift in identity may take place. The challenges of constructing a new identity and the pain of having to part with a familiar identity as part of a couple and as part of an intact family emerged as key issues in the interviews. This chapter will discuss literature on identity and women's identity options in Ireland. It will present and discuss the women's comments on the changes in identity that occurred as a result of separation.

Identity

The perspective taken in this study is that identity is socially constructed (Burr, 2003). Burr states that '[w]e are born into a world where the conceptual frameworks and categories used by the people in our culture already exist' (Burr, 2003: 7). Identity is formed by using these conceptual frameworks to make sense of the world and our place in that world. Burr states further that 'when people talk to each other the world gets constructed' (Burr, 2003: 8). Identity and sense of self are built during interactions between people.

Identity encompasses a personal self and a social self. A personal self is concerned with how individuals see themselves. A social self is concerned with how individuals think they are seen by others. Both conceptions of self may alter as a result of divorce (Gregson and Cayner, 2009). The person may begin to doubt themselves and their former positive conceptions of themselves as loveable, caring people. They may be concerned that others will start to see them as being in some way flawed or to blame because their relationship has broken down. Depending on the context, separation and divorce may be accompanied by a discourse of failure which may make it more difficult to emerge with a positive concept of self.

In Ireland and elsewhere marriage used to be seen as a woman's only opportunity to have a desirable life. 'There was a time when most stories about girls simply ended with marriage: the prince and princess married and lived happily ever after' (Bateson, 1989:101). Becoming a married woman or a nun or a 'spinster' used to be the only identities on offer for women in Ireland (O'Connor, 1998). The role definitions that women inherited in Ireland were shaped to fit a mainly rural world in which women had large families and did not work outside the home (Inglis, 1998). Prior to the 1960s, Irish women had few choices to construct a life that was different. There was little expectation that Irish women would have a life or an identity outside of the private sphere, outside of their roles as wife and mother. If they failed in their roles as wives, they had few positive role models to help them construct alternative identities.

Women who separate in midlife in Ireland are in a similar position to what Bateson describes as being 'on stage without a script ... working out courses through unknown landscapes' (Bateson, 2000:93). She asserts that 'when change affects one individual before it affects others, you see the ripples of turbulence but also the starting points of adaption and creativity at the margins' (p. 93). Irish women who separate are at the margins of a change in family structures and, as such, are bound to experience what Bateson calls 'ripples of turbulence' (p. 93). But they also have the opportunity to begin to be creative, to be resilient and to construct new discourses and understandings of separation. This is the challenge now facing Irish women who separate in midlife.

Finding 'Me'

The centrality of family identity for individual identity in an Irish context has already been discussed. Smart (2007) talks about the 'stickiness' of relationships with kin and how '[i]ndividual life trajectories are meaningful in the context of the other lives with whom they are linked' (p. 44).The women described how their lives had been linked with other people's lives, namely their parents, their grandparents, their siblings, their children, their in-laws, their spouses and how their identity and their sense of themselves had been largely defined by these relationships. The only lesson they are likely to have learned during their childhoods in Ireland was that separation was bad and that it signified failure.

Gertina van Schalkwyk (2005), in her study of South African divorced women, found that the point at which the women there began to reconstruct their identities was the point at which they could attribute some positive meaning to their past and present experiences and move on from using a discourse of failure about themselves for being divorced. Most of the women in this study are at a point where they can attach some positive meaning to their separation. For many of them the positive meaning has to do with finding themselves.

> ANNE: I've learned now that the most important relationship you have is with yourself and ... inner peace within myself.

> JANE: This has taught me, nobody knows what's going to happen tomorrow. What I've found I will never give up. Me. He might have his money and this girl he's with, but I have everything. Three beautiful daughters who love me to bits.

In the past, a married woman's entire identity and sense of self were defined by being a wife and mother. The two roles, wife and mother tended to be bundled together as if they were inextricably linked. Marital separation means that the roles and the identities that go with them have to be separated. Jane, in the quotation above, seems to be saying that her identity as a mother is more important than her identity as a wife.

Nora and Mary talk about how much they miss being part of a couple, how their established identity as part of a couple has had to shift, how there is no longer a 'we' and they have to become 'I' again.

> NORA: You miss being part of the couple. At the end of the day I have a pain in my heart. I have a hole in my heart. I just miss him, do you know. And I don't know will that eventually go away.

> MARY: I think that's the biggest thing, not having a companion, not having some-one to talk to about everything that's going on and concerns about your daughter.

Eileen, on the other hand, referred several times to how lonely and invisible she felt during her marriage and that it took time for her to realise that she could be her own person.

> EILEEN: I couldn't believe how I had suddenly gone from being this invisible person to having a voice. Suddenly I had a voice. I'm back in a world of my own, doing my own thinking. I'm beginning to realise that I am a person in my own right and that I'm not an appendage to everybody. I'm not an invisible person anymore. I'm me.

Geraldine seems to be at the point where she is comfortable with the status of being divorced and where she loves her new-found freedom but she acknowledges that it has taken her time to get to that point. As Bateson (2000) says, new beginnings do not happen overnight.

> GERALDINE: This whole separation is a journey and I have reached a stage in my journey that I am perfectly happy being single. I have no problem saying I'm divorced. It's not an issue for me. I'm much happier to be free, to be a free person, to be single. I really have found myself. I have found my wings at this stage. I am so happy about that. I love my freedom but it's not all a forward motion 'cos you get set-backs and you go back.

Sarah is also much happier to be separated than she was in her marriage. She regrets that she is less well-off financially than if she had stayed with her husband but she has no doubt that she is better off emotionally to have left. She likened being in an unhappy marriage to being in a con-centration camp.

SARAH: I don't like the fact that at my age, thinking of retirement in the next few years that I can't afford things but yet if I had to choose between before and now, now is much, much better!

L: You're in a better place?

SARAH: Oh God! I'm in the sunshine. I don't have that pain. I cried it out four years before I left, or even longer. I cried it out. It [the separation] was just tying it off, but it had totally died ... I was escaping. I used to think of the concentration camps, the men dig the tunnels out, how brave is that. You have to get out ... But there is that sense of relief, I can open the door and I can do whatever I want. I can be myself, I don't have to be putting on an act ...

Beck and Beck-Gernsheim (2002) talk about marriage as a trap and a denial of individual freedom of choice. Seen from this perspective, separation should mean liberation and freedom. The quotations above from Sarah, Geraldine and Eileen agree with that sentiment. Breda was very conscious that women in previous generations did not have a choice to leave their husbands and that by making that choice she was standing up for what she believed was her right, even though it involved a considerable amount of pain. She felt that being the mother of a child with special needs was a bigger part of her identity than being a divorced woman.

BREDA: I think it's always good to have choice ... and not to settle for second best ... There is gain and pain. When your back is to the wall, the gain is to actively choose what you want to do. Having to push through your own fears is a gain. Sometimes it's hard to see if the gains balance the pain. My hope is that the gains will go up.

L: How do you identify yourself now ... as separated, divorced, single again?

BREDA: I have a terrible identity crisis! ... An awful lot of my identity is tied up with being the mother of a child with special needs ... there is an extra added piece. I don't know who I would be without her. She is a huge part of my life. I have become the person I have become because of her. It is a bigger part of my identity than being divorced ... Being involved in setting up the support group happened after the divorce and is a huge part of my life now ...

Frances also initiated separation but speaks about how difficult she has found it and the devastating impact it has had on her. She also feels that very few people understand the pain involved because separated people hide their distress from almost everyone. They cope. They carry on. They distract themselves.

FRANCES: I kind of feel so shattered and battered and broken by it and nobody seems to notice because you can't go round with a long face on you. I suppose I distract myself but I know I'm distracting myself. I feel my heart is broken and that it can't be mended.

L: Is your self broken?

FRANCES: Yes and your confidence. I know that I'm still the same person but somehow or other it's left such a blow.

Several of the women (Catherine, Helen and Irene) talked about how they had survived the initial trauma of separating so suddenly and how they were adapting over time to the reality of being separated.

CATHERINE: And I am functioning. I'm functioning very well. I'm working, I've been on holidays. I really loved that. I know I can be okay but I'll only be okay.

HELEN: You have to try and make the best of it. I'm coming through it now. I feel that I myself was kind of put down for so long, I was never taken seriously or never considered first ... I think, you hit the wall loads of times but you don't ever go back as far as you were ... At the beginning I was terrified at the thought of being alone because the girls are moving on, that doesn't frighten me as much now.

IRENE: I am very much trying to get my own life back together. Two years on from separation has been a time of, probably for me, acceptance. Although I am hurt and I feel I've the scars on my face to show my sadness. I think I have accepted it. I just need to move on in life ... I'm a survivor definitely so I will survive ... There are people a lot worse off than me ... I'm not a person to close the curtains, put the lights off and stay in bed. I am very much one of these people that gets up and gets on with life and tries to put the best foot forward.

Catherine, Eileen and Irene had not chosen to be separated but they have come to see the benefits of being their own person. It is as if individualisation has been forced upon them and they are figuring out how to be individuals and how to enjoy living for themselves.

Bateson (1989) asserts that women spend their lives adapting to change and that 'constancy is an illusion' (p. 14). She points out that women spend their lives watching over the unfolding lives of their family and friends and when things change, they have the strength to adapt and to imagine something new. 'The central survival skill is the capacity to pay attention and respond to changing circumstances, to learn to adapt, to fit into new environments beyond the safety of the temple precincts' (p. 231). Women who separate are beyond the safety of the temple precincts in the sense that they may be alone facing into old age. Their prospects are both more open and less protected than before (Beck and Beck-Gernsheim, 2002). Following separation, they may have greater freedom to be their own person, but they may also be more vulnerable in that they no longer have the protection of their husband or his extended family, assuming the protection was there in the first place. Several of the women mentioned their fears about the future and growing old alone.

> BREDA: Now that I'm older, it is more frightening. You know, to cope on your own, being on your own, growing old on your own, how I am going to provide for myself? ... Waking up in the middle of the night sometimes ... nothing is secure ... Once you get over 50 you are on the down path.

> MARY: The thing I worry about is when my daughter moves on and I am living on my own in some small apartment that I'll become like some crazy old bag lady.

Bateson (2000) would contend that these women need to re-imagine their futures as a period of new beginnings rather than just as a period prior to old age. 'Through most of human history, adult work, marriage and child bearing meant that the dye was cast and fresh starts were a very rare luxury' (p. 102). Now, however, adulthood has become a longer period. It has more chapters than previously and separation can be just one more chapter.

Discussion: Identity Changes and Resilience

The women experienced various losses and gains during their journeys through separation. Many of their relationships had to be re-configured. They remained connected to their children and to their families of origin and friends but they disconnected from their former spouses and from many of the relationships which had been part of their married lives. Their identities as mothers, daughters, sisters, workers and friends remained largely intact. The loss of identity as part of a couple took time to come to terms with. The women had to construct new identities for themselves which involved losing their married status and embracing a 'single again' status. Having been part of a couple for more than half of their lives, it was difficult for some of the women to re-establish their sense of themselves as separate entities.

The women's comments refer to survival and resilience in the face of adversity. They range along a continuum from women who have integrated being separated into a positive sense of themselves, to those who can only see the negatives and the losses involved in separating and who are still very upset. Time is a factor, but it is not the only factor in arriving at a positive perception of the experience of separation. The women's personalities, the events that precipitated the breakdown of their marriages, their self-esteem, the strength of their other relationships and the support they received were some of the many factors that influenced their sense of well-being following separation.

CHAPTER 10

Experiences of Formal Support

In this chapter the fifth research question concerning the supports that the interviewees found most beneficial during the process of separation is addressed. Informal support from siblings, sisters in particular, parents, adult children, friends and work colleagues were identified as invaluable sources of support. The participants in the study also accessed formal support services. Their evaluation of the benefits of marriage counselling, mediation and legal advice services varied. This chapter presents data on the women's experiences of attendance at personal counselling and peer support groups. In order to provide a context for the discussion, public policy and literature on separation support are reviewed initially.

Types of Support

State Support

Public policy in Ireland tends to focus on families rather than on marriage (McKeown *et al.*, 2004). Support for families in which separation occurs is included within the general provisions and policies for family support services. Family support services are provided chiefly by the Department of Health and Children, the Health Service Executive and the Department of Social Protection and tend to focus on families with children under eighteen years of age (FSA, 2013). The Family Support Agency (FSA) was established in 2003 and had a lead role for ten years in providing mediation services and in allocating grants for marriage and relationship counselling services. In 2014 the FSA was incorporated into the new Child and Family

Agency, *Túsla*. The Mediation Service became the responsibility of the Legal Aid Board. The direction of this move would seem to indicate that the focus of the Mediation Service is primarily on legal matters, rather than on providing support to deal with the emotional aspects of separation.

The rationale for State support for families, in particular for families following separation, is that 'family relationships are universally acknowledged to have deep and enduring effects on the well-being of individuals and society ... and there is substantial evidence that children and adults can be significantly harmed when family relationships are not stable and healthy' (FSA, 2013: 10). Good marriages have been found to be 'more closely associated with adult well-being than almost any other variable' (p. 11). There is an onus, therefore, on the State to provide support for couples when problems initially arise in marriages, as well as during and after separation. The purpose of such support is to prevent the breakdown of marriage in the first instance, and if separation occurs, to provide support to minimise the negative effects on the well-being of the adults and children concerned. Research shows (p. 11) that the best predictor of a child's normal healthy development is the quality of interaction between a parent and child. Relationships between parents and children can be strained as a result of separation. Research also shows 'that separated and divorced adults have the highest rates of acute and chronic medical conditions and are at increased risk of admission to mental hospitals and committing suicide' (FSA, 2013: 11).

Apart from the Mediation Service, there are no state-run services whose primary function is to provide support for people who are separating. Marriage and relationship counselling services are provided by voluntary bodies. The services are partly funded by state grants under a scheme entitled *Scheme of Grants to Voluntary Organisations providing Marriage, Child and Bereavement Counselling Services*. In 2013, the scheme cost €8,147,000, roughly half of which was given to organisations providing marriage and relationship counselling (FSA Annual Report, 2013). The two main service providers at present in Ireland are *ACCORD* and *Relationships Ireland*. *Beginning Experience* is a smaller organisation which specialises in supporting bereaved and separated individuals. These are not the only organisations in Ireland providing support following separation but are the three organisations which were accessed by the women in this study.

ACCORD

The vision statement of *ACCORD* states that it is 'an agency of the Catholic Church providing a nationwide service to couples preparing for or seeking a deeper commitment within the sacrament of marriage' (<www.accord. ie>). *ACCORD* is the largest body in the country providing marriage education, enrichment and counselling services. There are fifty-eight centres nationwide with just under eight hundred volunteer counsellors and facilitators. All volunteers receive in-service training. Fees for counselling are charged on a sliding scale related to income.

There is no specific reference on the website to support being provided in relation to separation, although at least two of the women (Helen and Nora) attended *ACCORD* for counselling at the time of their separations and found the support to be beneficial. It is not clear whether Catholic-run marriage counselling agencies, such as *ACCORD*, see the provision of support in relation to separation as a key part of their mission.

Relationships Ireland (formerly MRCS)

Relationships Ireland was founded in 1962 and 'provides a range of services to those with problems in their personal relationships' (<www. relationshipsireland.com>). There is a specific section on their website entitled *Separation Support*. This section details counselling services for individuals/couples who are in the process of separation. The focus is on helping with the 'emotional impact of separation and divorce'. There is also a programme called *Teen Between* for teenagers whose parents are separating. *Post-Separation courses* are run regularly and are followed by on-going *Separation Support Groups*. The service is provided by trained counsellors. A sliding scale of fees operates. The service is only provided in Dublin. Catherine, Deirdre, Eileen, Irene, Sarah and Mary attended a

Post–Separation course in *MRCS* in November 2008, which is where initial contact with them was made.

Beginning Experience (B.E.)

Beginning Experience is a voluntary support group for bereaved and separated people. It was established in Texas by a Catholic nun, Sister Josephine Stewart and a divorced woman, Ms. Jo Lamia. 'The purpose of B.E. is to facilitate the grief resolution process for adults and children who have suffered a loss through death, divorce or separation, thereby enabling them to again love themselves, others and God' (<www.beginningexperience.org>). B.E. has a strong Catholic ethos. It currently operates in eight countries world-wide. The first B.E. programme was run in Ireland in 1986. The current activities include a six week course which takes place one evening per week, a residential week-end course and a follow-on four week, one night per week, course. The courses are copyrighted and are delivered by volunteers who are described as 'peer ministers' (<www.beginningexperience. org>). Courses run in Dublin, Cork, Dundalk and the West of Ireland. Initial contact was made with Breda, Frances, Geraldine, Helen and Kay at a B.E. residential week-end course in November 2008.

Research on Irish Support Services

Three studies on marriage and relationship counselling services in Ireland were reviewed for this study. O' Connor (2001) detailed a study carried out at Cork Marriage Counselling Centre. McKeown *et al.*(2002; 2004) described the findings of two studies carried out at ACCORD and MRCS.

O'Connor (2001) found 'that couples in later life struggle with marital unhappiness with equal frequency to couples in the early to middle years' (p. 7). Fifteen per cent of the clients surveyed were in either the 'launching the children' or the 'empty nest' stages of the family life-cycle. O'Connor recommended that agencies needed to target services towards older couples rather than concentrating predominantly on the earlier stages of marriage.

There were four times as many female clients attending the Cork service as male clients. Problems were 'fairly long-standing and often chronic' (p. 11) before people came for help. O'Connor reported that almost a third of those who came to counselling were already contemplating separation (p. 12). He suggested that marriage counselling, in the sense of wanting to work on and improve relationships, may not be what many clients are seeking when they come to marriage counselling agencies. He contended that 'supporting marriage must involve the support of separated and separating people' (p. 6) and that it might be necessary to develop a speciality in emotional mediation as a precursor to legal mediation. O'Connor drew attention to the importance of agencies serving all sections of the community and not providing exclusively for Catholics.

McKeown *et al.*(2002) surveyed in excess of 1,000 clients throughout Ireland who had attended ACCORD. They also completed a survey (2004) of 160 clients who used the services of MRCS. Couples that attended for counselling in both agencies tended to be middle-class and come from two-earner families. Women were more likely than men to attend (59% of clients were female) and to be the ones to initiate contact in relation to couples' counselling. Similar to the O'Connor (2001) study, the extent of marital unhappiness, particularly amongst women, was considerable at the start of counselling 'which implies that their marriages may be close to or even beyond breaking point' (p. 13). Eighty nine per cent stated that one of their goals in coming to counselling was to decide on the future of their relationships.

International Literature on Support following Divorce

In the USA, Amato and Wang (2000) conducted a longitudinal study over a 17 year period of 208 individuals who divorced. They set out to examine factors associated with adjustment to divorce. 'Adjustment was positively associated with (adequate) income, dating someone steadily, re-marriage, having favourable attitudes towards marital dissolution prior to divorce, and being the partner who initiated the divorce' (p. 655). They found that divorce adjustment was more difficult for older individuals than for younger individuals because 'older individuals, compared with younger individuals, have more invested (emotionally and financially) in their marriages and face bleaker prospects on the re-marriage market' (p. 666).

In a further article, Amato (2000) constructed a model called a 'divorce-stress-adjustment' model (Amato, 2000:1269). The main stressors identified for adults included sole parenting responsibility or loss of custody of children, loss of emotional support, continuing conflict with an ex-spouse and economic decline. The protective factors identified were individual resources, such as education, employment, income, friends, family, re-marriage, having a positive perspective on divorce and demographic factors such as gender, age, race and children. Amato suggested that these protective factors may help to moderate how the impact of divorce is experienced and may affect the level of adjustment that results. However, Amato (2000) concluded that 'people vary greatly in their reactions to divorce' (p. 1269). He argued that there is no easy way to predict how a separating individual will cope, recognising that the process of divorce adjustment is very individual and very complex (Amato, 2000).

Other studies on the support women found to be beneficial following separation expand on some of the 'protective factors' to which Amato refers. Henderson and Argyle (1985), from Oxford University, in the U.K., found that friends, specifically those who were not joint friends of a couple, as well as adult children were the most important sources of support. Steward and Clarke (1995), in a study of 116 separated women in Australia, found that esteem support, support that built a sense of self-worth, confidence and personal control were of most assistance. The importance of having a support network following divorce was emphasised. Smerglia et al. (1999), from the University of Akron in Ohio, USA, conducted a literature review and analysis of fifteen articles which were published between 1986 and 1998 on support following divorce. They also found that feeling understood, having someone to listen, someone to socialise with and someone who was emotionally supportive were the most beneficial types of support identified by women who were separated.

These findings emphasise, again, the emotional and social nature of the experience of separation for women and that it is in emotional and social areas that they most appreciate help.

Reluctance to Access Support

A point which was repeated several times during the interviews was that the women had told almost nobody about their marital problems. They had found it difficult to discuss their unhappiness with their husbands. Apart from some of them telling their sisters, the women were extremely slow to voice how worried they were about their marriages. Similar to findings by O' Connor (2001) and McKeown *et al.* (2004), in most cases the women were the ones to initiate marriage counselling. Anne, Deirdre, Kay and Mary attended some counselling sessions with their husbands. Most of the other women went alone because their husbands refused to attend. Eileen and Sarah's husbands initiated counselling following their wives' announcement that they wanted to separate, but by then it was too late.

> ANNE: A thing I have learned as well, I was a very independent person. I wouldn't have leaned on other people. I was too proud. Life isn't like that. People are there when you need them and vice versa. Hopefully, if anybody needs me in the future I will be there for them.

> GERALDINE: In my case, I didn't look for support. I was in denial for years. I suffered this and I carried this with me and I never asked for help from anybody. I went to one friend. I told her about it and she ran a mile.

The sensitivity with regards to acknowledging marital problems, the tendency to ignore them and hope they will dissipate on their own in time, and the reluctance to address them at an early stage through formal counselling would appear to be features of how Irish couples who are currently in midlife or older deal with serious difficulties in their marriages.

Counselling: Individual/Personal Counselling

The women accessed personal counselling in a variety of ways. Some attended private counsellors, others attended voluntary agencies and others were able to arrange counselling through *Employee Assistance* programmes in their work places. Services such as *Women's Aid*[1] and *Al Anon*[2] (Anne) were beneficial, as well as services such as *ACCORD, Relationships Ireland* and *Beginning Experience (B.E.)*. The point to emphasise is that anyone in this study who wanted counselling was able to access it.

> ANNE: Now *Women's Aid* were a huge help to me at the time when I was so vulnerable. They had counsellors there, like I was really in the throes of it at this time. It was the worst point. And I met a woman there who was so kind, who listened to me, who gave me such support.

Catherine, Frances, Irene and Nora attended just a few sessions with private counsellors. Their experiences varied. Catherine decided very quickly that counselling was not the type of support she needed, at that stage.

> CATHERINE: I went to see this guy twice and then I said 'look, I'm not coming to see you anymore. I'm paying a hundred euro to see you and I know it's a waste of time.' He said 'I'm so glad you said that ...'

Frances wanted help to understand why she was feeling so bad, given that she was the one to initiate separation.

> FRANCES: I went to a counsellor before I separated because I wanted perspective on this, 'am I making this to be bigger than it is?' After going for about six weeks, I had decided (with a little bit of direction) that separation was the best thing. And then we separated and after about six months I just went back to him ..., again for myself, because I wondered 'why do I feel this bad? Why do I feel all these emotions?' Then

---

1   Women's Aid is a voluntary organisation which provides support for survivors of gender-based violence.
2   Alcoholics Anonymous is a voluntary support group for those living with a person who misuses alcohol.

at one stage he said 'well, we really all have to move on'. And when he said that I just knew he was not the right counsellor for me.

Irene and Nora wanted to talk and to be listened to, but they also wanted some direction and some specific strategies to help them to cope.

> IRENE: A friend of mine had a friend who was a psychotherapist and I went along and she was a very nice person. We talked but after a number of sessions and money across the counter, which I couldn't really afford I said to her 'is there a structure on this or where are we going or what are you taking from this?' I'm probably one of those people that likes a little bit of structure on things. She said 'oh no, no, no, you're doing fine. I'm chatting to you and you're chatting to me' but I didn't feel I was getting pointers or whatever ...

> NORA: But I did go to a private counsellor for about six sessions ... All I did was speak to her like I'm speaking to you now or speaking to my friends. She just listened. She didn't give me any tips or any kind of ways to cope when you feel down.

For some of the women (Breda, Deirdre, Eileen, Geraldine, Helen, Sarah and Mary) long-term counselling was a very important support at all stages of the process of separating (See Appendix 2 for a summary on support). The women who initiated separation (Anne, Breda, Deirdre, Eileen, Frances and Sarah) all attended counselling prior to making the decision to separate. Attending counselling helped them to clarify what they needed to do.

> EILEEN: A counsellor that I had said 'you have to be true to yourself' and hearing that from a male and knowing I was being heard was huge. 'This is about you'. Suddenly I am the centre of this and it's ok for me to be the centre of my life. That was a huge impact.

Geraldine and Mary have been going to counselling for over five years and have found it hugely beneficial. Geraldine went to individual counselling at MRCS. Mary went to a private counsellor.

> GERALDINE: Professional counselling I would put as number one. It was down to the relationship I had with the woman who was counselling ... She and I worked together really well ... It started out being about my separation but as time went on she was my sounding board. Whatever was going on for me, whether it was Tom or work, my own parents, she'd talk to me about it. She'd guide me. Sometimes she gave me exercises to do. Sometimes she used things to help me work my way through

stuff. It was never directive. The whole thing was about coming around to see things for myself and that worked for me.

MARY: I still go to a counsellor myself from time to time and I find that is one of the best things ever because, although I have lots of sisters and they're great and very supportive, they're your family and they always want to tell you what to do. And sometimes you don't actually want someone to tell you what to do, you just want to tell someone and maybe have them ask you some questions to help you think about it …

The women in this study could afford to pay for private counselling. They could afford to travel to Dublin to access specialised separation support services. This may not be the case for the majority of Irish women who separate.

Peer Support/Groups

Twelve of the fourteen women (Jane and Anne being the exceptions) had been to post-separation courses either at *Relationships Ireland (formerly MRCS)* or *Beginning Experience.*

JANE: There was a support group, but I wasn't a separated women so I wasn't part of that … denial!

Anne had found peer support at Al Anon even though the focus was not specifically on separation.

ANNE: When I did go back to *Al Anon*, I had huge support from them. There were there for me, to listen. I found that great because you're with people who have been in similar situations and they understand and that's huge.
L: Did anybody suggest that you should try to save your marriage or that you should stick by your man?
ANNE: No, they didn't, not in *Al Anon*, because they knew my story all along, what I had been going through up to that and what the situation was.

Several of the women referred to the importance of peer support as they felt separation was an experience that could only truly be understood by those who had been through it.

BREDA: You don't understand something if you haven't been through it ... I would actually say it's not possible ... I heard about B.E. from one of my friends who separated. She was describing crying as she signed her separation agreement and saying that the only thing that helped her to get through it was the B.E. experience.

DEIRDRE: I don't think anyone who hasn't been through it can understand it. I don't tell everyone because my one fear is that if I start to tell everybody just how lonely I can get that they would be trying to call and I wouldn't want that. So I don't ever ... probably nobody really knows how lonely it gets and how difficult it was. Only people who have been through it understand that.

IRENE: I started to go to that weekend course in MRCS. I met some nice people there and I've kept contact with them and I've gone back every so often. You listen to other people's stories and their stories are ten times worse than mine. There are like-minded people going through a trauma. I know about that myself from work. Groups work. You always get something from it.

When Geraldine took her children to the *Rainbows*[3] Group, she and the other mothers went for coffee and started talking to each other while they were waiting for their children.

GERALDINE: The discovery that you could find support among peers in the *Rainbow* scenario was a complete revelation to me. That was a huge support to me even though we were all sort of grappling on our own at a very emotional stage. We could still talk openly to each other. It was there I realised that there are other people like this that you can talk to and be as open as you like and they're not going to go off blabbing to somebody else because they've got a similar story and I'm not going to be blabbing their business to anybody else either ...

Eileen and Frances stated that they had no family members or close friends who were separated so they knew no one who could explain the experience to them. Frances stated how misunderstood she felt and how the pain she was feeling was not acknowledged.

3   Rainbows is a programme for children going through bereavement or parental separation.

EILEEN: I'm just thinking I have no friend who is separated or divorced so I have nobody to talk to, to find out. There is nothing. I had to go looking. I saw an ad in the paper for this weekend down in Dublin for a married and separated counselling service ... We all had the same experience in that we were out of our marriages but I had nobody to tell me what it was going to be like beforehand. There was nobody to tell me. It is very much virgin territory.

FRANCES: I remember thinking if you do express anything, that gives the idea that you are resentful or bitter. And you can't express yourself for fear that that's how you might be interpreted ... Another thing I hear a lot is 'there are so many people separated now that nearly everybody is separated'. You're meant to feel better because there's an awful lot of people separated. Actually none of my friends are separated and my family aren't and like there's nobody in my circle who is separated. Anyway, that's not the point if the whole city is separated. It's how they feel about how you feel.

Geraldine, Helen and Kay initially attended the six week *Coping Programme* run by B.E., followed by the residential week-end and have trained to be volunteer peer counsellors with the organisation.

GERALDINE: This *Beginning Experience*, I saw the ad. I read it. The boss told me about it ... I didn't want to talk about it. I put it away and didn't look at it again for a year ... I went on my own to *B.E. Coping Programme* in September 2006 and I'm still in it. I'm actually on the Dublin Board of B.E. now. I've been involved with them ever since. It has been one of the best things that I could ever do ... I suppose you have to be in a place in your head first of all to look for the support and then to be able to look for the right type of support for you ... Like B.E is really supportive and I'm glad I found it but I only found it by chance. People don't know about it and it isn't everywhere. It's not like if you lose your partner through death, there's all kinds of bereavement groups available and people really open their arms to you and welcome you in ... People can understand the whole thing about losing somebody through death ... We lose our friends, our brothers, our sisters, our partners. So you can kind of relate to that but not everyone can relate to the whole separation thing. It's just too icky for people to take a hold of.

It is interesting to note that Geraldine waited a year after hearing about B.E. to begin attending the *Coping Programme*. It seems that people choose different types of support at different stages in the process of separation. Initially they seem to turn to sisters, friends and personal counsellors. It takes time for people to be ready to attend groups.

Summary of Experiences of Counselling

According to the women in this study, the models of emotional support and advice following separation provided by *B.E.* and *Relationships Ireland* were very beneficial. The women found meeting others who were separated to be particularly helpful. Those who lived in Dublin were able to attend programmes over an extended period. Those who lived outside of Dublin attended week-end courses and were not able to establish the same type of supportive network as those living in Dublin. *ACCORD* is the only nation-wide service available for couples in distressed marriages but its mission is marriage preparation and enrichment rather than support following separation. There would appear to be a need to extend post-separation support services outside of Dublin.

Private counselling is the sector to which the women turned. All of them were able to access private counsellors. Some of them (Kay) expressed concern about how unregulated the sector is and about how it is can be difficult to find the 'right' person (Geraldine). Cost was a factor for some in decisions not to continue counselling. The women's evaluation of the service they received varied. The 'success' of the counselling experience seemed to depend very much on the relationship the women developed with their particular counsellor. The women (and their husbands) needed to believe in the process. They needed to engage with it. They needed to feel understood. They needed to feel respected. Where these things were present, counselling 'worked', where they were missing it did not 'work'. Like the women in the Steward and Clarke (1995) study in Australia, support that built a sense of self-worth, confidence and personal control was found to be most beneficial by the women in this study.

Pointers for Designing Formal Support Services

As Amato (2000) stated, adjustment to divorce is very individual and very complex. Different supports will work for different people. Some women may get adequate support from family and friends and not require access to formal support. Others find that family and friends are only helpful 'up to a point' (Breda, Geraldine, Frances and Helen) because they have no personal experience of separation. A range of formal separation support services needs to be available. Points made by the women about the factors that contributed to the breakdown of their marriages, their experiences of separation and the supports they found beneficial are helpful when considering the manner in which support services might be organised, as the following points suggest:

- There should be more emphasis at an early stage on teaching young people relationship skills. The study shows that communication difficulties, problems with showing love and care, and problems with resolving conflict contributed to the breakdown of the women's marriages. These are skills which can be taught (McKeown *et al.*, 2004).
- The study also pointed to a gulf in understanding between men and women, between men's 'worlds' and women's 'worlds' and an inability to bridge that gap. The women felt they were lacking in assertiveness skills. They suggested that their husbands lacked the ability to discuss emotional or relational issues. The persistence of traditional gender role stereotyping (O'Connor, 2015) in the socialisation of Irish boys and girls is a matter that requires further attention.
- *Marriage Preparation and Marriage Enrichment* courses in Ireland are provided mainly by Catholic-run organisations. There needs to be a broader range of service providers involved in these courses than is the current practice.
- Additional support is required to help couples in the transition to parenthood. Several of the women identified this stage as being difficult, particularly when they tried to combine it with full-time employment.
- The practice of delaying attendance at marriage counselling services until relationships are in serious trouble was very evident in the study. It is imperative that any barriers to attendance be removed or minimised. If a Catholic ethos is a barrier, non-denominational services could be provided in more locations. If cost is a barrier, the cost should be on a sliding scale related to income.
- Negative attitudes to counselling created a barrier to accessing help in distressed marriages. By the time many of the couples in this study

attended counselling, one person had already left the marriage. A change of mind-set is required to make it more acceptable to both men and women to address problems with the help of a professional at an early stage.

- If problems cannot be resolved to the satisfaction of both parties, or if problems appear to be resolved but continue to recur, couples may benefit from assistance to separate, sooner rather than later. This study shows that women delayed separating and lived in very unhappy situations for decades, to the detriment of their health. (It is not clear how this suggestion will affect children, but that topic is beyond the scope of this study.)
- Separation support needs to become part of the skill set of all agencies which provide marriage counselling. Research (Aronson *et al.*, 2003) shows that where separation can be agreed upon, relationships post-separation tend to be less problematic and divorce adjustment tends to be more positive.
- Once separation occurs, more professional specialised services are necessary to support couples and their children with the emotional aspects of separation. State Mediation Services which focus primarily on legal issues are inadequate on their own.
- The current level of expenditure by the Government on this sector is insufficient. It is no longer appropriate to assume that Catholic agencies will provide all services that relate to marriage throughout the country. Services such as *Relationships Ireland* and *Beginning Experience* have limited availability outside of Dublin, which means that women in rural Ireland have very limited access to on-going peer support groups.
- Leaving the private-for-profit personal counselling sector responsible for providing emotional support is somewhat problematic because the sector is not yet state-regulated, local counsellors may not have specialised expertise in dealing with separation and cost may be pro-hibitive for low-income families.

The range of support services suggested may not appeal to every woman who is separated but formal services are necessary for the occasions when professional help is required. In most stressful situations, people can turn to their family and friends for support and advice. In the situation of marital separation in Ireland, this may be unfamiliar territory for family and friends. Several of the women stated that they were the first ones in their families to separate and that all of their friends were still married. Notwithstanding this, informal support emerged as the most beneficial source of support on a daily basis. It is important, therefore, that there is greater understanding of the emotional process of separation, not just by professionals but also by the general public, as informal support is key to how adults and children cope with separation. The hope is that this book will contribute to deepening that understanding.

CHAPTER II

Concluding Comments

The purpose of this study was to explore the experiences of Irish women who separate in midlife and to give 'voice' to a cohort of women who have previously been invisible. The bulk of the writing consists of excerpts from interviews with fourteen Irish women who are separated. The aim is to generate discussion and deepen understanding on the part of professionals and the general public so that appropriate support can be provided for women in this situation. This chapter contains summaries of the data as they relate to the five research questions posed at the outset of the study.

Impact of Family and Cultural Attitudes to Separation

The influence of traditional attitudes to separation can be seen in the fourteen women's accounts of their experiences of separation. The women who initiated separation delayed the decision to separate for years, decades in some cases, partly because they had internalised a belief that separation was wrong and because they prioritised their children's needs over their own. Despite being extremely unhappy, they felt for years that they did not have sufficient grounds to end their marriages. They felt that a stigma still attached to separation and that their children would be hurt and shamed by being from a 'broken home'. They felt their parents would be upset. They had been brought to prioritise family needs over individual needs and found it very difficult to behave in a way that went against those beliefs and practices. For most of the women, it went against their beliefs and values to prioritise their own needs and to make the decision to separate.

Embeddedness in traditional beliefs about lifelong marriage impacted in many of the same ways on the women who had not initiated separation. These women also talked about feeling guilty about having failed to save their marriages. They blamed themselves for failing to pick a man who would be faithful. They blamed themselves for failing to keep their husbands sufficiently happy. They blamed themselves for letting their children down by failing to maintain an 'intact' family. Some of them felt like failures because they were the first ones in their families or in their group of friends to separate. The first set of beliefs about separation they had to confront and challenge were their own beliefs.

All of the women felt pain and regret that their marriages had ended. Many of the women retained elements of older belief systems about the ideal of life-long marriage and struggled to replace a discourse of failure in relation to separation with a more positive meaning of the place of separation in their lives. The combination of continuity with past belief systems and change towards the integration of newer, more liberal perspectives are common themes in discussions on social change in Ireland (Share *et al.*, 2012; Connolly, 2015). The dominant view of separation as being entirely negative may have shifted, but residual elements of that negative perspective remain which impact on the way in which many Irish women who separate in midlife experience separation.

Even though divorce has been legal in Ireland since 1997 and the numbers separating and divorcing have continued to increase, for many of the women who participated in this study, separation was not a normative experience. They are amongst the first generation of Irish women to have to accept and acknowledge that their marriages have broken down. Apart from four women who had siblings separated, most of the women had few role models amongst their families or their friends to show them how to 'do' separation. They lived in 'respectable' families in which separation was not supposed to happen. It is not necessarily that they have been made to feel like failures or are stigmatised by their family and friends but that the sense of shame is internalised. People may have liberal views about the right to separate, but it is another matter when the person separating is themselves. In order to cope, it is necessary for the women to stop blaming themselves and stop feeling ashamed. It is also necessary for them to change their own construction of separation from the negative view they have grown up with to a more positive construction of separation which they can integrate into their lives for the future.

Processes and Events that Lead to Separation in Midlife

When writing about the individualisation thesis, Beck and Beck-Gernsheim (2002) contended that women used to abandon their dreams when they got married but that, in more recent times, women hold onto their dreams and abandon their marriages. The suggestion is that women have higher expectations of relationships and, if these expectations are not fulfilled, they leave their marriages and search for fulfilment, often in another relationship. This sentiment was not borne out in this study by the women who initiated separation. A desire for individualisation was not their motivation for separation. For most, maintenance of physical and mental health was the reason for initiating separation. They feared that their health would deteriorate if they continued to live with the level of unhappiness they felt within their marriages. They battled with the decision for years and only separated when they felt their relationships were beyond repair.

All of the participants in the study recounted stories about relationship difficulties which had been building for years. They talked about unresolved problems with the transition to parenthood, problems with sharing childcare and household tasks, differences over money and sex, difficulties with resolving conflict, a lack of emotional reciprocity, problems with communication and an absence of support during times of crisis as all being factors which contributed to their eventual separations.

The common theme running through all of the stories was the theme of not feeling loved. Feeling loved, in this context, does not just refer to romantic love. It refers to feeling that the work needed to sustain love is not being done. The person who does not feel loved withdraws in order to protect themselves from further hurt, as in the case of the women who initiated separation. These women did not feel loved but they did not separate in order to find love with another man. The six women whose husbands had affairs were left not knowing exactly why their husbands had been unfaithful. The women could track patterns in their relationships which could have contributed to their husbands' feeling that their wives no longer loved them but, in the absence of interviews with the husbands, it is not possible to say with any certainty why the men ended their marriages in the way they did.

It is clear from the stories the women told that some of their relationships had broken down long before separation actually took place. Other relationships, from the women's perspective at any rate, were still 'good enough' up to the point at which they learned that their husbands were having affairs. The suddenness with which separation was triggered is worthy of note and may explain some of the pain and trauma felt during the separation process. The women who initiated separation blurted it out without any warning. Some of the men who disclosed having affairs only told their wives on the day they were planning to move in with their girlfriends.

It is not clear from the data why there was such gulf in perception between the men and the women about their respective levels of unhappiness within their marriages. Part of the explanation may be that men and women who are now in midlife were socialised to live in different spheres, a private sphere for the women and a public sphere for the men, and that, even though many of the women had entered the public sphere by being engaged in paid employment, a gap still existed between men and women in this age group about their respective roles within the private sphere of marriage. Some of the men were clearly embedded in traditional gender roles and only occasionally helped with childcare and household tasks. Where the women expected these jobs to be shared, since they were also going out to work, there were problems.

Embeddedness in traditional roles also seems to have manifested itself in the couples' inability to communicate about emotional issues. Some of the women had been brought up to be quiet and non-assertive. Some of the men had been brought up to be strong, silent types. It was just not done in their generation to discuss difficult emotional matters. This inability by both parties to communicate openly and at a deep level resulted in huge gaps in understanding between spouses which eventually led to their separations.

Losses and Gains

Separation entails coming to terms with a series of losses. The women in this study referred to the loss of identity as part of a couple, loss of an intact family, loss of a familiar routine, loss of joint friends, loss of a lifestyle, loss of a shared future, loss of a secure income, possibly the loss of a family home and, in general, the loss of self-esteem. They had been married for between twenty and thirty-five years. Separation entailed losing much of what had been familiar to them for more than half of their lives.

A consistent finding in the literature reviewed is that women are less well-off financially as a result of separation. Women in their forties and fifties who have been out of the workforce for extended periods due to child-minding responsibilities often find it difficult to find work. Women who are older also have fewer years in which to provide for retirement and many have inadequate pension provision due to having fragmented employment histories. The women who gave up full-time work to care for their children are struggling to find employment and are facing into retirement without occupational pensions. While some maintenance arrangements were made for dependent children, almost no allowances were allocated for the women. The emphasis in the courts is on future needs rather than on taking past caring roles or opportunities to work outside the home into account. This emphasis leaves women who have stayed at home to mind their children very vulnerable in the event of separation. The presumption that women who are in midlife can find employment and provide for themselves does not take into account their contribution to the accumulation of family resources in the past or the barriers, including ageism and the need for re-training, that they may face in returning to the workforce in the future.

The majority of the women interviewed for this study, nine out of fourteen, have professional qualifications and worked full-time during their marriages. In this respect they are atypical of many women their age in Ireland. The women are all less well off financially than if they had stayed married but could not be described as being in poverty. Those who had to buy their husbands' share of family homes will have mortgages until they are seventy. They will not be able to afford to take early retirement and, at a time of their lives when they thought they would be financially secure, their standard of living has been diminished significantly.

In terms of accommodation following separation, nine of the fourteen women remained in the same family homes with their children. Some of the women stated that remaining in the family home was a 'mixed blessing'. They referred to the expenses involved in maintaining older houses. Some of them were still providing for young adults who returned home intermittently and were not financially independent. For most of the women, being able to stay in their family homes and continuing to provide a home base for their children was something they valued. The courts may have seen their home purely as an asset which could be sold but the women saw it as providing stability and continuity for themselves and their children at a time of upheaval in their lives. Other women felt differently about their homes. They associated them with a life they had lost and felt the houses were filled with memories they wanted to get away from. They felt that a fresh start in a new house would help them to 'move on' and be part of their establishing a newly independent identity.

Separation potentially entails not only a change in accommodation and lifestyle but also a change in identity. The women described how confused they felt at no longer being part of a married couple and the fear they felt for a future on their own. They felt that a large part of the person they had been and the lifestyle they had lived for over twenty years had been lost as a result of separating. The only identity many of them associated with being separated had negative connotations that symbolised failure and a broken home.

Along with the losses felt by the women during the process of separation, they also identified gains they had made. The main gains they referred to entailed discovering themselves again. Most of the women seem to have arrived at a point where they were able to envisage new opportunities and to assign more positive meanings to their future lives. They discovered that they had a voice, that they were resilient, that they could cope on their own with whatever transpired in their lives, that they could maintain a stable home base for their children, that they could build new friendships and construct a new life for themselves. They referred to how important it was to have retained their own friends, their work and their own interests during the course of their married lives because they had those to rely on when they separated.

Building a new social life seems to have been particularly difficult for many of the women. For them, it was not so much that they were excluded from the social group of which they had been apart during their married lives but that they absented themselves from it. In small communities where there was the possibility of being in the company of their ex-husbands if they continued to attend the same venues and events, the women removed themselves. At the time of the interviews, none of the women had entered a new relationship. They stated that their social lives tended to revolve around their sisters and female friends. They were open to the possibility but were not optimistic about their chances of meeting another life-partner.

Family Practices following Separation

Much of the literature reviewed on family practices post-separation focuses on parenting. Almost all of the interviewees had teenagers or young adults at the time of their separations so no court rulings were made in relation to access or custody. As is usual in these cases, most of the children continued to live with their mothers. Some mothers felt that their relationships with their children had become closer following separation. Others felt their relationships had become strained due to on-going problems in communication with their children's fathers. A striking finding about contact between children and their fathers is how many adult children refused to have anything to do with their fathers. In four of the fourteen families surveyed, one or all of the children refused to have any contact. This amounted to eight out of a total of thirty-five children who opted to have no communication with their fathers. (In one family where the mother was the person to initiate separation and leave home, the children initially would have nothing to do with their mother.) Difficulties between fathers and children seem to have centred on fathers being involved in new relationships and some children not being prepared to involve themselves with their fathers' new partners. Nine out of fourteen of the women have little or no contact with their husbands/ex-husbands. Only three out of fourteen families have celebrated family events together.

Patterns established during marriages carried over into post-separation practices and relationships. Couples who could not communicate during their marriages did not suddenly figure out how to communicate after they separated. The data show that issues between spouses remained unresolved for years during their marriages and continued to be unresolved during their separations, with the added barriers to communication of feelings of rejection and attribution. The couples did not have the skills or the inclination to put the work into trying to negotiate new relationships with their ex-spouses. For most of them, a 'clean break' seemed like the easiest and least stressful solution.

However, the notion of a 'clean break' goes against the ideal of an amicable/harmonious separation which is presented in discourses on how to separate. Some of the women said they felt blamed for not making their children speak to their fathers and for not inviting the fathers to family events. To the women it was self-evident that their marriages had broken down because they did not get on with their husbands or because their husbands were having affairs. Many of them keep up the appearance of being 'happily married' for years for the sake of their children and their families. They were not prepared to pretend to be 'happily separated' just to satisfy a norm to which they did not subscribe.

The earlier discussion about embeddedness in family and cultural beliefs about marriage and separation may help to explain why so few of the couples in this study had amicable separations. There may be a generational factor at play here. These women were brought up to believe that family based on marriage was the most important aspect of a woman's life and that it was a woman's job to take care of it. Some of those who initiated separation believed this and delayed separating for years. Those who did not initiate separation struggled to come to terms with losing what to them was a cornerstone of their lives. While the women may be resilient enough to re-construct their lives and to cope on their own, it appears that, for most of the non-initiators at any rate, establishing amicable relationships with spouses who hurt and rejected them is just too much to expect.

Experiences of Support

On a daily basis, informal support from family and friends was the most valuable assistance the women received. However, because marital separation was outside most Irish people's experience, understanding of the complexity of separation and of the overwhelming intensity of emotions that accompanied it was limited. All of the women needed and were able to access professional counselling. An excellent range of separation support services was provided by *Relationships Ireland* and *Beginning Experience*. The peer support aspect was found to be particularly beneficial. The difficulty is that there is very limited availability of these services outside of Dublin.

The only State-funded nation-wide service in existence specifically designed to support separating couples is the Mediation Service. The focus of this service is primarily on avoiding court hearings by assisting couples to reach agreement on access to children, housing and financial arrangements. Eight out of the fourteen interviewees used the service. Two managed to reach agreements. The expectation that couples who are in the process of a break-up can calmly agree on complex financial and custody issues seems unrealistic, unless support is also provided to deal with the emotional aspects of the process. The legal aspects of marital separation do not constitute the entirety of the experience of separation. Findings from this study would indicate that the emotional aspects are of far greater importance but receive less attention or funding.

There is still a legacy in Ireland of leaving matters relating to families entirely in the hands of the Catholic Church. As the number of people separating increases and as the number of practising Catholics decreases, funding to provide a range of separation support services throughout the country will need to be expanded.

Final Messages

None of the women in this study found the journey through separation easy. It was accompanied by a series of major losses in their lives with which they are still coming to terms. However, the study showed clearly that the processes and the outcomes of separation were different for different women. Some are 'in the sunshine' (Sarah), 'have found their voice' (Eileen) and are 'much happier to be free, to be a free person, to be single' (Geraldine). Other women are coping and functioning but carry the scars of the hurt they have been through, as Frances says 'I kind of feel so shattered and battered and broken by it and nobody seems to notice because you can't go round with a long face on you.'

This study captures not only the practical outcomes of separation, in terms of income and accommodation, but, more importantly, it captures the emotions the women felt during the various stages of the separation process. It is important to capture the emotions behind the figures and to provide a space in which women can be heard. The sense of loss experienced as part of the process of separation must be acknowledged. The sense of loss is related to the centrality of marriage in this generation of Irish women's lives. The support they found most beneficial was support which built their self-esteem. The message the women conveyed is that just because separation is more common, does not mean that it is less painful. There is a danger that the shift to normalising separation and to expectations of being able to 'move on' quickly and establish amicable relationships with ex-spouses will result in the emotionally difficult aspects of separation being diluted and silenced.

The manner in which this age group of Irish women are 'doing' separation is a function of both their past and present lives. It is unlikely that future generations of women will experience separation in quite the same way as this age cohort of women. It was important to capture this experience at this point in time. The study ends on a positive note with all of the women saying that they have found the entire process of separation difficult, but that they will survive and grow stronger and re-build their lives around relationships with their children, with their family and friends and, most importantly, with their newly found selves.

References

Ahrons, C. R. (2005) 'Divorce: An Unscheduled Family Transition' in B. Carter and M. Mc Goldrick (eds) (2005) *The Expanded Family Life Cycle*, (3rd edition), Boston: Allyn and Bacon Classics.

Amato, P. A. (1994) 'The Impact of Divorce on Men and Women in India and the United States', *Journal of Comparative Family Studies*, 25.2.

Amato, P. A. (2000) 'The Consequences of Divorce for Adults and Children', *Journal of Marriage and Family*, 62 (Nov. 2000): 1269–1287.

Amato, P. A., and Previti, D. (2003) 'People's Reasons for Divorcing: Gender, Social Class, the Life Course and Adjustment', *Journal of Family Issues*, 24: 602.

Amato, P. A., and Wang, H. (2000) 'Predictors of Divorce Adjustment: Stressors, Resources and Definitions', *Journal of Marriage and the Family*, 62: 655–668.

Andreb, H., Borgloh, B., Brockel, M., Gisselmann, M., and Hummelsheim, D. (2006) 'Causes and Consequences of Divorce: Cross-national and Cohort Differences, an Introduction to this Special Issue', *European Sociological Review*, 22.5: 533–560.

Aronson, E, Wilson, T.D., and Akert, R.M. (2003) *Social Psychology*, 4th edition, New York: Prentice Hall.

Australian Institute of Family Studies (2000) 'Australian Divorce Transitions Project', *Family Matters*, 55, autumn (<www.aifs.org.au>).

Bacik, I. (2004) *Kicking and Screaming: Dragging Ireland into the 21st Century*, Dublin: O'Brien Press.

Barry, U. (2008) *Where are we now? New feminist perspectives on women in contemporary Ireland*. Dublin: Tasc at New Ireland.

Bateson, M. C. (1989) *Composing a Life*, New York: Grove Press.

Bateson, M. C. (2000) *Full Circles, Overlapping Lives (Culture and Generation in Transition)*, New York: Random House.

Beale, J. (1987) *Women in Ireland*, Dublin: Macmillan.

Beck, U. (1992) *Risk Society: Towards a New Modernity*, London: Sage.

Beck, U., and Beck-Gernsheim, E. (1995) *The Normal Chaos of Love*, Cambridge: Polity.

Beck, U., and Beck-Gernsheim, E. (2002) *Individualisation*, London: Sage.

Bernard, J. (1982) *The Future of Marriage*, New Haven: Yale University Press.

Bernardes, J. (1997) *Family Studies: An Introduction*, London and New York: Routledge.

Berry, D. B. (1998) *The Divorce Sourcebook*, Cambridge: Lowell House.

Binchy, W. (1984) *Marriage Breakdown*, Dublin: Veritas.

Bogolub, E. (1991) 'Women and Mid-life Divorce: Some Practice Issues', *Social Work*, 36.5.

Bowlby, J. (1983) *Attachment* (2nd edition), Tavistock Institute, London: Basic Books.

Brady, Cardinal S. (2009) 'The Family as the Foundation of Society' in H. Bohan (ed) (2009) *Family Life Today*, Dublin: Veritas.

Breen, R., and Cooke, L.P. (2005) 'The Persistence of Gendered Division of Domestic Labour', *European Sociological Review*, 21.1: 43–57.

Brody, H. (1974) *Inishkillane, Change and Decline in the West of Ireland*, New York: Schocken.

Brown, S., and I-Fen Lin (2012) 'The Grey Divorce Revolution', Working Paper, Bowling Green: Bowling Green State University.

Bryman, A. (2004) *Social Research Methods*, New York: Oxford University Press.

Buehler, C., and Legg, B. (1993) 'Mothers' receipt of Social Support and their psychological well-being following Marital Separation', *Journal of Social and personal Relationships*, 10:21–38.

Burley, J., and Regan, F. (2002) 'Divorce in Ireland: The Fear, the Floodgates and the Reality', *International Journal of Law, Policy and Family*, Vol.16, pp. 202–222.

Burr, V. (2003) *Social Constructionism* (3rd edition), London: Routledge.

Byrne, A., and Lentin, R. (2000) *(Re)searching Women*, Dublin: I.P.A.

Carsten, J. (2004) *After Kinship*, Cambridge: Cambridge University Press.

Carter, B., and McGoldrick, M. (eds) (2005) *The Expanded Family Life Cycle*, (3rd edition), Boston: Allyn and Bacon Classics.

Cheal, D. (2002) *Sociology of Family Life*, Basingstoke: Palgrave.

Central Statistics Office (2007) *Census 2006, Principal Demographic Results*, Cork: C.S.O.

Central Statistics Office (2011) *Men and Women in Ireland 2010*, Dublin: Stationery Office.

Central Statistics Office (2012) *This is Ireland – Highlights from Census 2011*, Part 1, Dublin: Stationery Office.

Central Statistics Office (2012) *Profile 5 Households and Families* Dublin: Stationery Office.

Clarke, L., and Berrington, A. (1999) *Socio-demographic predictors of divorce*, (<www.oneplusone.org.uk>).

Clear, C. (2001) *Women of the House: Women's Household Work in Ireland 1922–1961*, Dublin: Irish Academic Press.

Coen, M. (2008) 'Religious Ethos and employment equality: a comparative Irish perspective', *Legal Studies* 28.3: 452–474.

Coleman, L., and Glenn, F. (2009) *When couples part: Understanding the consequences for adults and children* (<www.oneplusone.org.uk>).

Commission on the Status of Women (1973) *Report of the First Commission on the Status of Women*, Dublin: Stationery Office.

Conneely, S. (2002) *Family Mediation in Ireland*, Aldershot: Ashgate.

Connolly, L. (2003). *The Irish women's movement: From revolution to devolution*, Dublin: Lilliput Press.

Connolly, L., and O'Toole, L. (2005) *Documenting Irish Feminisms: The second wave*, Dublin: Woodside Press.

Connolly, L. (ed)(2015) *The 'Irish' Family*, New York: Routledge.

Considine, M., and Dukelow, F. (2009) *Irish Social Policy. A Critical Introduction*, Dublin: Gill & Mc Millan.

Coulter, C. (1997) 'Goodbye Daddy, Hello Divorce' in A. Bradley and M.G. Valiulis, (1997) *Gender and Sexuality in Modern Ireland*, Amherst, MA: University of Massachusetts Press.

Coulter, C. (2008) *Family Law in Practice: A Study of Cases in the Circuit Court*, Dublin: Clarus Press.

Delphy, C., and Leonard, D. (1992) *Familial Exploitation: A New Analysis of Marriage in Contemporary Western Societies*, Cambridge: Polity.

De Roiste, A. (2006) 'The Family: A Systems Perspective', in T. O'Connor, M. Murphy (eds) *Social Care in Ireland*, Cork: C.I.T.

De Vaus, D. (2004) *Diversity and Change in Australian Families: Statistical Profiles*, published by The Australian Institute of Family Studies (<www.aifs.gov.au>).

Dillon, M. (1993) *Debating Divorce: Moral Conflict, in Ireland*, Lexington: The University Press of Kentucky.

Dooney, S., and O'Toole, J. (1998) *Irish Government Today*, Dublin: Gill & Macmillan Ltd.

Dowd, P. (2006) *A Swift Pure Cry*, Oxford: David Fickling Books.

Dronkers, J., Kalmijn, M., and Wagner, M. (2006) 'Causes and Consequences of Divorce: Cross-National and Cohort Differences' *European Sociological Review*, 22.5,: 479–481.

Duck, S. (1998) (3rd edition) *Human Relationships*, London: Sage.

Election Literature 1995 <www.irishelectionliterature.wordpress.com>.

Erwin, K. (2007) 'More disputes could go to mediation', *Family Law Matters*, 1.3: 58–60.

Eurostat <www.eurostat.ec.eu/statistics>.

Fahey, T., and Field, C. A. (2008) *Families in Ireland*, Dublin: Government Publications Office.

Family Support Agency (2013) *Strategic Framework for Family Support* (<www.tusla. ie>).

Ferriter, D. (2004) *The Transformation of Ireland 1900–2000*, London: Profile Books Ltd.

Ferriter, D. (2009) *Occasions of Sin: Sex and Society in Modern Ireland*, London: Profile Books Ltd.

Finch, J., and Mason, J. (1993) *Negotiating Family Responsibilities*, London: Tavistock/ Routledge.

Finch, J., and Mason, J. (2000) *Passing On: Kinship and Inheritance in England*, London: Routledge.

Fine-Davis, M. (2011) *Attitudes to Family Formation in Ireland*, Dublin: Trinity College.

Fischer, T., deGraaf, P. and Kalmijn, M. (2005) 'Friendly and antagonistic contact between former spouses after divorce: Patterns and Determinants', *Journal of Family Issues*, 26: 1131–1163.

Fisher, B., and Alberti, R. (2006) *Rebuilding when your Relationship ends* (3rd edition), Atascadero: Impact Publishers.

Fisher, B., and Tronto, J. (1990) 'Towards a Feminist Theory of Care' in E. Abel and M. Nelson (eds), *Circles of Care*. Albany, NY: State University of New York Press.

Fitzgerald, G. (1973) *Towards a New Ireland*, Dublin: Torc Books.

Giddens, A. (1992) *The Transformation of Intimacy*, Cambridge: Polity.

Giddens, A. (2006) *Sociology* (5th edition), Cambridge: Polity.

Gillies, V. (2003) *Family and Intimate Relationships: A Review of the Sociological Research*, London, Families and Social Capital ESRC Research Group, South Bank University.

Gilligan, C. (1982) *In a Different Voice*, Cambridge, MA: Harvard University Press.

Gillis, J. (1996) *A World of their own Making: Myth, Ritual and the Quest for Family Values*, Cambridge, MA: Harvard University Press.

Gillis, J. (2004) 'Gathering Together', in A. Etzioni and J. Bloom (eds) *We are what we celebrate: Understanding Holidays and Rituals*, New York: New York University Press.

Government of Ireland (1937) *Bunreacht na hÉireann*, Dublin: G.P.O.

Gregson, J., and Creynar, M. (2009) 'Finding 'Me' Again: Women's Post Divorce Identity Shifts', *Journal of Divorce and Remarriage*, 50: 564–582.

Harding, S. (1987) *Is there a feminist methodology?* Bloomington: Indiana University Press.

Henderson, M., and Argyle, M. (1985) 'The Source and Support given to Women at Divorce/Separation', *British Journal of Social Work*, 15:57–65.

Hill, M. (2003) *Women in Ireland: A Century of Change*, Belfast: Black Staff Press.

Hilliard, B. (1995) 'Changing Perspectives in the Sociological Study of the Family', in I. McCarthy (ed) *Irish Family Studies*, Dublin: UCD Press.

Hilton, J. M., and Anderson, T.L. (2009) 'Characteristics of Women with Children who Divorce in Midlife compared to those who remain Married', *Journal of Divorce and Remarriage*, 50: 309–329.

Hogan, D., Halpenny, A.M., and Greene, S. (2002) *Children's Experience of Parental Separation*, Dublin: Children's Research Centre, Trinity College.

Holland, M. (1985) 'Why the Flynn case is so important' in A. Bourke, S. Kilfeather, M. Luddy, M. Mac Curtain, G. Meaney, M. Ni Dhonnchada, M. O'Dowd and C. Wills, in *The Field Day Anthology of Irish Writing (2002) Irish Women's Writing and Traditions*, Vol. 5 (eds) Cork: Cork University Press in association with Field Day.

Hume, M. (2007) 'Unpicking the Threads: Emotion as central to the Theory and Practice of Researching Violence', *Women's Studies International Forum*, 30.

Hussey, G. (1993) *Ireland Today: Anatomy of a Changing State*. Dublin: Town House and Country House.

Inglis, T. (1998) *Moral Monopoly*, Dublin: UCD Press.

Inglis, T. (2003) *Truth, Power and Lies: Irish Society and the Case of the Kerry Babies*, Dublin: UCD Press.

Inglis, T. (2005) 'Origins and Legacies of Irish Prudery: Sexuality and Social Control in Modern Ireland', *Eire-Ireland*, 40:3 and 4, Fall/Winter 2005: 9–37.

Inglis, T. (2007) 'Catholic Identity in Contemporary Ireland: Belief and Belonging to Tradition', *Journal of Contemporary Religion*, 22. 2: 205–220.

Inglis, T. (2008) *Global Ireland: Same Difference*. New York: Routledge.

Irish Election Literature (1995) <www.electionliterature.ie>.

Irish Family Mediation Service <www.fsa.ie>.

Irish Statute Books, <www.irishstatutebooks.ie>.

Irish Times, <www.irishtimes.com>.

Joint Committee on Marriage Breakdown (1985) *Report of the Joint Committee on Marriage Breakdown* (1985), Dublin: G.P.O.

Kalmijn, M. (2010) 'Country Differences in the Effects of Divorce on Well-Being: The role of Norms, Support and Selectivity', *European Sociological Review*, 26.4: 475–490.

Kavas, S., and Gunduz-Hosgor, A. (2011) 'It is Not a Big Deal, I Can Do it Too' Influence of Parental Divorce on professional Women's marital Experience in Turkey, *Journal of Divorce and Remarriage*, 52.8: 565–585.

Kenny, M. (2003) 'Forty Years On', *Studies*, 92.365 (Spring, 2003):7–12.

Kennedy, F. (2001) *From Cottage to Creche*, Dublin: I. P. A.

Kiely, G. (1989) *Finding Love*, Dublin: Poolbeg Press.

Kiely, G. (1998) 'Marriage and relationship counselling in a changing society' in Final Report of the Commission on the Family (1998) *Strengthening Families for Life*, Dublin: Minister for Social Community and Family Affairs.

Kittay, E. (2002) 'Love's Labor Revisited' *Hypatia*, 17.3: 237–250.

Kubler-Ross, E. (1997) *On Death and Dying*, (Reprint edition) New York: Scribner.

Kusgen McDaniel, A., and Coleman, M. (2003) 'Women's Experience of midlife Divorce following long-term Marriage', *Journal of Divorce and Remarriage*, 38.3/4:103–128.

Lawler, S. (2002) 'Narrative in Social Research' in T. May (ed), (2002) *Qualitative Research in Action*. London: Sage.

Legal Aid Board (2014) *Family Mediation* (<www.legalaidboard.ie>).

Lowenstein, L. F. (2007) *Parental Alienation: how to understand and address Parental Alienation resulting from acrimonious Divorce*, Lyme Regis: Russell House Publishing Ltd.

Lunn, P., Fahey, T., and Hannan, C. (2009) *Family Figures: Family Dynamics and Family Types in Ireland, 1986–2006*, Dublin: ESRI and UCD.

Lupton, D. (1998) *The Emotional Self*, London: Sage.

Lynch, K. (1988) 'The ethos of girls' schools: an analysis of differences between male and female schools', *Social Studies* 10.1/2:11–13.

Lynch, K. (1999) *Equality in Education*, Dublin: Gill and Macmillan.

Lynch, K. (2007) 'Love Labour as a distinct and non-commodifiable form of care labour'. *The Sociological Review*, 55.3: 550–570.

Lynch, K., and Lyons, M. (2008) 'The Gendered Order of Caring' in Barry, U. (2008). *Where are we now? New feminist perspectives on women in contemporary Ireland*. Dublin: Tasc at New Ireland.

McDaniel, A., and Coleman, M. (2003) 'Women's Experiences of Midlife Divorce Following Long-Term Marriage', *Journal of Divorce and Remarriage*, 38.3/4.

McCafferty, N. (1985, reprinted 2010) *A Woman to Blame: Kerry Babies Case*, Cork: Attic Press.

McCormick, J. (2008) *Understanding the European Union*, Basingstoke: Palgrave.

McDonnell, A. (1999) *When Strangers Marry: A Study of Marriage Breakdown in Ireland*, Dublin: Columbia Press.

McGinnity, G., and Russell, H. (2008) *Gender Inequalities in Time Use: The Distribution of Caring, Housework and Employment among Women and Men in Ireland*, Dublin: E.S.R.I.

McGréil, M. (1997) *Prejudice in Ireland Revisited*, Maynooth: Survey and Research Unit, St Patrick's College, Maynooth.

McGoldrick, M. (2005) 'Women through the Family Life Cycle' in B. Carter and M. Mc Goldrick (eds) (2005) *The Expanded Family Life Cycle*, (3rd edition), Boston: Allyn and Bacon Classics.

McKay, S. (2008) 'Introduction' to Barry, U. (2008). *Where are we now? New feminist perspectives on women in contemporary Ireland*, Dublin: Tasc at New Ireland.

McKeown, K., Lehane. P., Rock, R., Haase, T., and Pratschke, J. (2002) *Unhappy marriages: Does Counselling help?* Accord <www.accord.ie>.

McKeown, K., Pratschke, J. and Haase, T. (2003) *Family Well-Being: What Makes a Difference*, Report, Shannon: Ceifin.

McKeown, K., Haase, T. and Pratschke, J. (2004) *Distressed Relationships: Does Counselling Help*, Dublin: MRCS.

Mahon, E. (1994) 'Ireland-A Private Patriarchy', *Environment and Planning*, A, 26, 1994, pp. 1277–1296.

Mahon, E., and Moore, E. (2011) *Post – Separation Parenting: A study of separation and divorce agreements made in the Family Law Courts of Ireland and their implications for parent-child contact and family lives*, Dublin: Government Publications.

Marital Breakdown: A Review and proposed Changes (undated) Pi 9104 Dublin: Stationery Office.

Martin, F. (2002) 'From Prohibition to Approval: The Limitations of the 'No Clean Break' Divorce Regime in the Republic of Ireland', *International Journal of Law, Policy and Family*, 16: 223–259.

Mason, J. (2002) 'Qualitative Interviewing: Asking, Listening and Interpreting' in T. May (ed.) (2002) *Qualitative Research in Action*, London: Sage.

May, T. (1997) (ed.) *Social Research: Issues, Methods and Process*, Buckingham: Open University Press.

May, T. (2002) *Qualitative Research in Action*, London: Sage.

Maynard, M., and Purvis, J. (1994) *Researching Women's Lives from a Feminist Perspective*. London: Taylor and Francis.

Montenegro, X., Fisher, L. and Gross, S. (2004) 'The Divorce Experience: A Study of Divorce at midlife and beyond', Report, *AARP The Magazine* (May 2004).

Moore, E. (2010) *Renegotiating Family Practices Post Separation; An Irish Case Study*, PhD Thesis submitted to Trinity College, Dublin.

Morgan, D. (1985) *The Family, Politics and Social Theory*, London: Routledge and Kegan Paul.

Morgan, D. (1996) *Family Connections*, Oxford: Polity.

Morgan, D. (2002) 'Sociological Perspectives on the Family' in A. Carling, S. Duncan and R. Edwards (eds) *Analysing Families: Morality and rationality in policy and practice*, London and New York: Routledge.

Nestor, J. (2006) *Irish Family Law*, Dublin: Gill and McMillan.

Parad, H., and Parad, L. (2005) *Crisis Intervention Book 2:The Practitioner's Sourcebook, for Brief Therapy*. Tuscon, AZ: Fenestra Books.

Oakley, A. (1999) 'People's ways of knowing: gender and methodology' in S. Hood, B. Mayall and S. Oliver *Critical issues in Social Research: Power and Prejudice*, Buckingham: Open University Press.

Oakley, A. (2005) The *Ann Oakley Reader: gender, women and social science*. Cambridge: Polity Press.

O'Brien, M. (2008) *The Irish Times: A History*, Dublin: Four Courts Press.

O'Brien, M., and Rafter, K. (eds) *Independent Newspapers – A History*. Dublin: Four Courts Press.

O'Carroll, G. (2007) *The Sheriff. A Detective's story*, Edinburgh: Mainstream Publishing Company (Edinburgh) Ltd.

O'Connor, A. (1999) 'The Kerry Babies Mystery', *Sunday Independent* 29 November 1999. <www.independent.ie>.

O'Connor, C. (2001) 'Marital Counselling Research Project', <www.fsa.ie>.

O'Connor, P. (1998) *Emerging Voices: Women in Contemporary Society*, Dublin: Irish Institute of Public Administration.

O'Connor, P. (2015) 'A premature farewell to gender?' in Connolly, L. (ed) *The 'Irish' Family*, Oxan and New York: Routledge.

O'Hara, L. (2011) *When a Relationship Ends: Surviving the Emotional Roller-Coaster of Separation*, Dublin: Orpen Press.

O'Hara, P. (1997) 'Women in Farming Families: Shedding the Past and Fashioning the Future' in A. Byrne and M. Leonard (eds) *Women and Irish Society, A Sociological Reader*, Belfast: Beyond the Pale Publications.

O'Mahony, E. (2010) *Practice and Belief among Catholics in the Republic of Ireland; A summary of data from the European Social Survey Round 4 (2009/2010) and the International Social Science Programme Religion III (2008/2009)*, Irish Bishops Conference. <www.catholicbishops.ie>.

Parsons, T., and Bales, R. (1955) *Family, Socialization and Interaction Process*, New York: Free Press.

Rhoades, H. (2002) 'The non-contact mother' *International Journal of Law, Policy and Family*, Vol.16, pp. 87–94.

Rusbult, C. E., Yovetich, N. A., and Verette, J. (1996) 'An interdependence analysis of accommodation processes', in G. J. O. Fletcher & J. Fitness (eds), *Knowledge structures in close relationships: A social psychological approach* (pp. 63–90), Mahwah, NJ: Erlbaum.

Sakraida, T. (2005a) 'Common Themes in the Divorce Transition Experience of Midlife Women', *Journal of Divorce and Remarriage*, 43.1/2: 69–88.

Sakraida, T. (2005b) 'Divorce Transition Differences for Midlife Women', *Issues in Mental Health Nursing*, 26: 225–249.

Scuka, R.F. (2015) 'A Clinician's Guide to Helping Couples Heal from the Trauma of Infidelity', *Journal of Couple and Relationship Therapy*, 14:141–168.

Sevenhuijsen, S. (1998) *Citizenship and the Ethics of Care*, London and New York: Routledge.

Shatter, A. (1997) *Family Law* (4th edition) Dublin: Butterworths.

Share, P., Corcoran, M., and Conway, B. (2012) *Sociology of Ireland*, Dublin: Gill and MacMillan.

Sheehan, G., and Fehlberg, B. (2000) 'Families, divorce and family law', *Family Matters* 55, Autumn 2000, Australian Institute of Family Studies.

Sigle-Rushton, W. (2010) 'Men's Unpaid Work and Divorce: Reassessing Specialisation and Trade in British Families', *Feminist Economics*, 16.2: pp. 1–26, Research by the London School of Economics.

Silva, E.B., and Smart, C. (1999) (eds) *The New Family*, London: Sage Publications.

Smart, C. (1984) *The Ties that Bind: Law, Marriage and the Reproduction of Patriarchal Relations*, London: Routledge and Kegan Paul.

Smart, C. (1999) 'Divorce in England 1950–2000: A Moral Tale', CAVA workshop Paper 2.

Smart, C. (2004) 'Changing Landscapes of Family Life: Rethinking Divorce', *Social Policy and Society*, 3: 401–408, Cambridge University Press.

Smart, C., and May, V. (2004) 'Why can't they agree? The underlying complexity of contact and residence', *Journal of Social Welfare and Family Law*, 26. 4: 347–360.

Smart, C. (2005a) 'Changing Commitments: A study of Close Kin after Divorce in England', in M. MacLean (ed.) *Family Law and Family Values*, Oxford: Hart Publishing.

Smart, C. (2005b) 'Textures of Family Life: Further Thoughts on Change and Commitment', *Journal of Social Policy*, 34.4: 541–556.

Smart, C. (2007) *Personal Life: New Directions in Sociological Thinking*. Cambridge: Polity.

Smart, C., and Neale, B. (1999) *Family Fragments ?* Cambridge: Polity.

Smart, C., and Shipman, B. (2004) 'Visions in Monochrome: Marriage and the Individualisation Thesis', *Sociology*, 55.4: 491–509.

Smerglia,V., Miller, N., and Kort-Butler, L. (1999) 'The Impact of Social Support on Women's Adjustment to Divorce: A Literature Review and Analysis', *Journal of Divorce and Remarriage*, 32.1/2.

Spencer, L., Richie, J., O'Connor, W. (2003) 'Analysis: Practices, Principles and Processes' in J. Richie and J. Lewis *Qualitative Research Practice: A Guide for Social Science Students and Researchers*, London: Sage.

Stanley, L., and Wise, S. (1993) *Breaking Out Again*. London: Routledge.

Steward, J., and Clarke, V.A. (1995) 'The Role of Social Support in ameliorating Stress in Separated Women with Children', *Australian Journal of Psychology*, 47. 3:164–170.

Subotnik, R, and Harris, G. (2005) *Surviving Infidelity: Making Decisions and Recovering from the Pain*, (3rd edition) Avon, MA: Adams Media.

Thomas, C., and Ryan, M. (2008) 'Women's Perception of the Divorce experience: a Qualitative Study', *Journal of Divorce and Remarriage*, 49.3/4.

Timonen, V., Doyle, M., and O'Dwyer, C. (2009) *The Role of Grandparents in Divorced and Separated Families*, Dublin: Family Support Agency.

Tovey, H., and Share, P. (2000) *A Sociology of Ireland*. Dublin: Gill & Macmillan.

Trinder, L. (2008) 'Maternal Gate Closing and Gate Opening in post-divorce Families', *Journal of Family Issues*, 29: 1298–1324.

Uhlenberg, P. Cooney, T., and Boyd, R. (1990) 'Divorce for Women after Midlife', *Journal of Gerontology*, 45.1:S3–S11.

Uunk, W. (2004) 'The Economic Consequences of Divorce for Women in the European Union: The Impact of Welfare State Arrangements', *European Journal of Population* 20: 251–285.

Van Schalkwyk, G. (2005) 'Explorations of Post-Divorce Experiences: Women's Reconstructions of Self', *ANZJFT*, 26, 2:90–97.

Vatican, *Humanae Vitae* <www.vatican.va>.

Weston, R., and Smyth, B. (2000) 'Financial Living Standards after Divorce', *Family Matters* No.55 Autumn 2000, Australian Institute of Family Studies.

Whelan, C., and Fahey, T. (1994) 'Marriage and Family' in C. Whelan (ed) (1994) *Values and Social Change in Ireland*, Dublin: Gill and Macmillan.

Wineman, D. (1999) 'Divorce: Its Impact on the older female' Doctoral Dissertation, Institute for Clinical Social Work Chicago.

Wolcott, I., and Hughes, J. (1999) 'Towards understanding the reasons for divorce', Working Paper 20, Australian Institute of Family Studies.

Worden, J. W. (1991) (2nd edition) *Grief Counselling and Grief Therapy*, London: Tavistock.

Appendices

Appendix 1: Thematic Framework for the Study

1. Family of origin/Childhood

1.1   Location (rural/urban)
1.2   Size of family
1.3   Father's occupation
1.4   Mother's occupation
1.5   Religious observance
1.6   Education (own and siblings)
1.7   Issues in family (illness, death ...)

2. Awareness of Separation during Childhood

2.1   No knowledge
2.2   Happened to celebrities
2.3   Happened to foreigners who lived here
2.4   Happened to Irish who lived abroad
2.5   Other family members separated
2.6   Awareness of unhappy marriages
2.7   Other

3. Leaving Home Stage

3.1   Occupation
3.2   Study

3.3   Migration/travel
3.4   Courtship
3.5   Pregnancy
3.6   Pre-marital sex
3.7   Other

4. Marriage and Parenthood

4.1   Timing/number of children
4.2   Experience with first child
4.3   Resentment/contentment with division of tasks
4.4   Impact of work/lack of work
4.5   Quality of couple relationship
4.6   Method of resolving conflict
4.7   Sexual relationship
4.8   Significant events (death/illness of parents/holidays)

5. Events/Processes Leading to Separation

5.1   Attempts at counselling
5.2   Previous separations
5.3   Emotional infidelity
5.4   Sexual infidelity
5.5   Woman as initiator/ reasons
5.6   Blurting it out/ moving out
5.7   Initial reactions of husband
5.8   Initial reactions of wife
5.9   Initial reactions of children

6. Life After Separation

6.1	Legal settlements
6.2	House
6.3	Income/maintenance
6.4	Relationship with ex
6.5	Mother's relationship with children
6.6	Father's relationship with children
6.7	Family events
6.8	Social life/ new partners
6.9	Other (Making sense of separation)

7. Supports

7.1	Family reaction/support
7.2	Friends as supports
7.3	Work colleagues as support
7.4	Counselling
7.5	Mediation
7.6	B.E./M.R.C.S. attendance
7.7	Other supports

Appendix 2: Relationships following Separation

No.	Process around Separation	Relationship With Ex	Children	Mother's Relationship With Children	Father's Relationship With Children	Family Events	Social Life	Attitude to Re-partnering
1	Wife left due to issues around his drinking	'No contact at the moment'	1 under 18, 1 over 18	Daughter left with mother. Son sees mother	Daughter sees father. Son stayed with father	Would not attend events jointly at present	Likes to travel with friends and sisters. Has friends in Al. Anon. and in work	'I don't know if I want a man. It's not on the agenda right now'
2	Wife left because 'he would not meet her half way on anything'	'We rarely talk to each other'	2 over 18, 1 with special needs	Daughter with special needs lives with mother. Son in his 30s stays in contact	Daughter sees her father. Son had already left home. Wanted to 'stay out of separation'	2 children spend Christmas with mother	'Not so much that I lost friends as that I removed myself. I went back to college'	'Absolutely no interest. I have not gone back dating. I still love him'. (Husband has new partner)
3	Pattern of emotional infidelity. When she raised the issue, he left	'I see him on and off'	3 over 18. Left home	Almost daily contact with children	Close contact. 'Love him but could never trust him'	Attend some events together. She feels upset afterwards	'I always had my own circle of friends. Have lost some friends who were joint friends. Have stopped having people over to the house. One couple, I see her but not him'	'I wouldn't rule out having another relationship but I'm not there yet. I want a relationship with my husband. It is too hard to let go'

No.	Process around Separation	Relationship With Ex	Children	Mother's Relationship With Children	Father's Relationship With Children	Family Events	Social Life	Attitude to Re-partnering
4	Husband and wife had become distant. Wife asked him to leave. He agreed	'He is nicer to me now … but I'm not relaxed in his company'	1 PhD student 1 due home from Australia	Children spend periods of time in family home with mother.	Children see their father when they are home	'He comes over for Christmas'	'Not having friends in the same situation is my biggest problem. Friends are still in their marriages. Very upsetting not to have anyone to go on holidays with. I need new friends'	'In the beginning I said never again. Now I'd love the company but I would never want to marry'
5	Wife left. She felt controlled and invisible	'At the moment I don't want anything to do with him'	3 left home 2 postgrads	Children very angry with mother. One girl maintained contact in the first year. More contact with others recently	Children supported father because 'he has no one else'	She went back for Christmas. Will not go back again	'I moved to an area where I knew nobody … but I have gained socially'	
6	He wanted to sell up and move away. She did not want to leave. Relationship had become fraught	'I haven't spoken to him since this time last year'	3 adults (1 single mother and child living with wife)	Children were 'matter of fact' about the separation. They have regular contact with mother	Very little contact with children. 'He wanted to get away from all responsibility'	He was invited but did not come for Christmas	Lots of friends but misses the friendship with her husband	'I don't know about anyone else because I suppose I still love x. It's possible but I wouldn't do the marriage thing'. (Husband has new partner)

No.	Process around Separation	Relationship With Ex	Children	Mother's Relationship With Children	Father's Relationship With Children	Family Events	Social Life	Attitude to Re-partnering
7	He left to move in with another woman	'I don't talk to him'	3 children in third level	Three sons living with mother. She feels her relationships with them have got closer	The two younger boys see their father about once a month. The oldest boy will not see him	Father not invited	Has separated friends in work and in B.E.	'I'm not looking for another man to pay the bills. I would love to experience the closeness of a strong relationship. It would have to be a rich widower but they want younger women.' (Husband has new partner)
8	Wife discovered evidence that he was having an affair. Asked him to leave	'I haven't actually spoken to him in three years'	2 in third level 1 recent Masters graduate	'We have become really close, the four of us'	Only the youngest girl will see her father	Father not invited by the girls to conferrings, debs, 21st	'Very hard to socialise with previous couple friends'. Goes out with women friends and friends from B.E. 'Have to push yourself, easy to sit in'	'If I met somebody, fine, but I would never again depend on somebody completely'. (Husband has new partner)
9	He said he was leaving. It transpired that he had met another woman	'Unless it's something official, I don't want anything to do with you'	3 in third Level education	Children very supportive of their mother. They live with her	They were very angry with their father. They meet him sporadically. They are not okay with meeting his new partner	Father not involved in family events	'Have not felt lonely because my kids are there all the time'. Has sisters. Walks a lot	'I loved being in a relationship. I'm not sure that it will happen again or that I will allow it to happen.' (Husband has new partner)

No.	Process around Separation	Relationship With Ex	Children	Mother's Relationship With Children	Father's Relationship With Children	Family Events	Social Life	Attitude to Re-partnering
10	Wife suspected emotional infidelity. When she questioned him, he denied it but said he did not love his wife and left	'We don't even talk now'	1 in third level 2 working	Three girls are very close to their mother. They spend weekends and holidays with her	'There's no relationship with his children'. The girls refuse to see him	Father not invited to family events, including upcoming wedding	'I want to start socialising but I can't afford to'. Has lost some joint friends connected with his sporting interests but still has her own friends	'I'm terrified'. Kissed a man but afraid of getting hurt. (Husband has new partner. 'This is the fourth woman since he left me')
11	The husband said he needed to leave in order to have space to sort himself out	'He finds it very distressing meeting me, so he won't meet me'	1 in third level 1 working in London	Son and daughter became distant from mother initially. Relationships are good now	The daughter 'loves him but knows he is not to be relied on'. The son never had a good relationship with him. Both children are willing to see their father but he makes infrequent contact	He was invited to a conferring but does not want to come	'Socially I have found it very difficult'. She lost a social life that was connected to his interest in sport and music. She has an entirely female circle of friends now	'I'd love to meet another man but I'd be very slow to do anything'. (Husband has new partner)
12	There were difficulties about intimacy and affection in this marriage from the start. The wife left	'I don't mind meeting him. He is the one who has a huge problem'	2 in third level 1 working	The girls were angry at their mother initially. They are more understanding now	The middle girl stayed with her father to finish her Leaving. They go between houses	They have been to graduations together. The girls divide Christmas day between parents	'We were living separate lives before I left'. She used to socialise with work friends so that stayed the same	

No.	Process around Separation	Relationship With Ex	Children	Mother's Relationship With Children	Father's Relationship With Children	Family Events	Social Life	Attitude to Re-partnering
13	Wife said she was relieved when her husband announced he was leaving	'He can come and go here, to pick her [daughter] up no problem'	1 child in secondary school	Mother and daughter live together. They would have a 'pretty good relationship now'	He was still fighting with his daughter until recently. Relationship has improved	Daughter does not want parents together for any events	She lost friends due to migrating. They did not build a joint social life in Ireland because they were having such trouble in their relationship. She has friends for activities during the day but night time is more difficult	'Wish I could find someone. I called up a dating agency but I am too old'. Worried about becoming a 'crazy old bag lady'. (Husband had a new partner but that relationship has ended)
14	He talked in terms of his 'pathway' with his wife and children being at an end and that he needed to be with a new woman who was his 'soul mate'	'I meet him occasionally but find it very upsetting'	1 in third level 1 working	The girls are very supportive of their mother	Girls do not want to see their father	Girls do not want to invite him	She lost people who were his friends but has plenty of friends of her own. She hates going places where it is all couples	'If there was another man in my life I think I could move on a lot faster. Just somebody to give me a hug'. (Husband has been involved with another woman)

Appendix 3: Support following Separation

No.	Family as Support	Friends/Work Colleagues	Counselling	B.E MRCS Mediation	Other Support activities
1	Two sisters gave brilliant support. They supported her decision to leave and helped her in practical ways to stay out	Two very good friends who could not have done more. Very supportive boss	Women's Aid Employee Assistance	9 mediation sessions did not lead to an agreement	Al. Anon. gave me the strength and the courage
2	Mam elderly. Sister very ill. Not much support	Separated friend was supportive. Made new friends in college and in support group for parents which she set up	Private counselling ongoing	Separated friend told her about B.E. 'You don't understand something if you haven't been through it'	
3	Support from his family. Her sister and brother were 'wonderful'	'My boss is my friend. I had a network of friends I could fall back on'	Previous counselling for the family/couple	MRCS	Entered a triathlon, doing a parachute jump. Took a photography course
4	Her mother was very slow to tell anyone. 'She was probably ashamed'. Her sisters were supportive. They were the only ones she had told she was unhappy in her marriage	'It would have been a huge scandal in work in the past but not now. People were very supportive'	Previous counselling	MRCS. Nobody knows how lonely it gets or how difficult it was. Only people who have been through it understand. Mediation worked	
5	Her sister was her main support. Her brother's spouse took her husband's side	Two friends helped. Had only told one person about her unhappy marriage	Counsellor said 'you have to be true to yourself. It is okay to be at the centre of your own life'	MRCS Agreement not reached in mediation	Walking by the sea

No.	Family as Support	Friends/Work Colleagues	Counselling	B.E MRCS Mediation	Other Support activities
6	Little support from family. Relationships not that close		She went to private counselling to help clarify if separation was the right option	B.E. – Would not go back 3 sessions of mediation attended. He felt the female mediator was biased against him and would not go back	
7	'Brother great. Parents devastated. Separation did not fit in with their norms and values but they did not disown me'. Referred to it as her situation'	'I said it straight away in work and when I met my friends. Friends were supportive but they did not know what to say'	Individual counselling at MRCS for 5 years	'B.E has been one of the best things I could ever do. Five of us who met there are like sisters'. Is on the Board of B.E. Started mediation but did not continue?	She attended a course called 'The Art of Effortless Living' in Wicklow. It was about letting go and just being
8	Support from parents and siblings 'up to a point'. 'They did not really understand'	Friends were supportive but they did not really understand because they had not been through it	She went to Accord. Found it very helpful. He would not attend	'Mediation was a disaster'. B.E. helped something to shift. Trained as a facilitator at B.E.	
9	'My sisters, my single sister in particular, have been my rock of strength. She's better than any husband'	Have good work colleagues	Few sessions. Was costing money. No clear pointers given on how to cope. She stopped going	'Met some nice people at MRCS weekend course. Have gone back to other sessions. Have stayed in touch with a few people'	Found a Practical Philosophy course very beneficial. Have affirmations stuck up around the house and the car. Count my blessings
10	'My parents are the best. They felt rejected as much as I did. He was their son'	'I have five solid friends and my family and my neighbours. All their numbers are beside my bed'	Yes – see section on 'previous attempts at counselling' (5.1)		

No.	Family as Support	Friends/Work Colleagues	Counselling	B.E MRCS Mediation	Other Support activities
11	Her parents have been very good. They organised her sisters to be with her on a rota basis. Sisters were marvellous. Brothers have provided practical help	Friends were fantastic as were in-laws. Boss in work was 'absolutely wonderful'. Work helped	Didn't trust the counselling process. Peer support is better than one to one counselling	'B.E has helped to normalise separation by being able to talk about it normally. The service has been incalculable'	
12	Two sisters were very helpful. 'His family would blame me'	'I have lots of friends at work'	Counselling in Accord (see section 5.1)	MRCS Private mediation for three sessions. Then State service. It was not a difficult one	
13	Sisters were great, particularly older separated sister. Not that brothers were not great but 'you don't really talk about all that stuff with your brothers'	'Friends were good but I didn't really discuss my problems with them'		Attended MRCS course. Wanted to meet people going through the same thing who would be available to socialise with	Plans to go back to do a Masters
14	'Mam is very helpful, ringing all the time and sending a few pounds'. Sisters are helpful too but 'I don't tell them the full extent. They have their own troubles'	'I have three or four great friends'			Attending a Psychiatric Day Service Has tried hypnosis

Index